DO NOT PASS THE PARCEL

SARA NOOR

Contents

Preface ix
Introduction xi

Part One

Chapter 1 3
Chapter 2 5
Chapter 3 7
Chapter 4 9
Chapter 5 11

Part Two

Chapter 6 15
Chapter 7 18
Chapter 8 20
Chapter 9 23
Chapter 10 27
Chapter 11 29
Chapter 12 31
Chapter 13 33
Chapter 14 35

Part Three

Chapter 15 39
Chapter 16 42
Chapter 17 44
Chapter 18 46
Chapter 19 48
Chapter 20 50
Chapter 21 53

Part Four

Chapter 22 57
Chapter 23 59
Chapter 24 62

Part Five

Chapter 25   67
Chapter 26   70
Chapter 27   76
Chapter 28   80
Chapter 29   83

Part Six

Chapter 30   89
Chapter 31   91
Chapter 32   92
Chapter 33   93
Chapter 34   97
Chapter 35   99

Part Seven

Chapter 36   107
Chapter 37   109
Chapter 38   111
Chapter 39   113
Chapter 40   116
Chapter 41   119
Chapter 42   121
Chapter 43   122
Chapter 44   127
Chapter 45   131

Part Eight

Chapter 46   137
Chapter 47   139

Part Nine

Chapter 48   143
Chapter 49   147
Chapter 50   157

Part Ten

Chapter 51   163
Chapter 52   166
Chapter 53   169

Chapter 54   171
Chapter 55   175

Just in Case   181
Acknowledgments   189
Notes   193

Dedicated to all the women and mothers, particularly to those who die in childbirth – whose death is not marked with a public holiday – who are not buried with an honour – whose coffin is not wrapped in flags – who don't win medals for their sacrifice – whose death is not seen as the loss of a hero – whose name is not used to name places – who just silently die – whose death is nothing but a number – who are referred merely as *another woman died.*

Preface

I did not write this book; this book made me write it. To say *I* did or did not write it connotes a deliberate action, but that was not the case. It might be more appropriate to say that "this book chose me to be the person to write it".

To make it simple, let me explain what actually happened. I was standing in my kitchen, alone, doing what needed to be done for the next meal or so, when this idea knocked me from inside. I felt this deep urge and gushing need to reach out for pen and paper. Next, I saw myself sitting on my bed with a diary and pen; I was writing it. This is exactly how it began.

And then it kept coming: while cleaning the floor, while folding the laundry, while wiping the kitchen counter-top, while packing lunches. It even woke me up at night. It kept coming to me in small and big chunks.

This phenomenon is called "Aamad" in Urdu, when one receives an impulsive message or inspiration from nature and feels prompted to action that message. That is what I just did.

I was chosen. I felt like it came to me and politely asked, "Would you be willing to join me?" And I said, "Yes please," with tearful eyes. I had been a barren land for years … inspiration hadn't come for years … it was like a long-awaited raindrop in the desert.

Introduction

This book has been written in the pure cultural context of Pakistan. References have been made to Islamic rules and verses. However, it aims to address all the communities of the world where similar social norms and cultural values are shared, and it aims to address all the women and mothers out there. One of the main areas of discussion is the impact of cultural and social limitations on the lives of migrants, and that's what makes it relevant here, or maybe everywhere.

There are a few things that I would like to say in the beginning: this book is based on true events and stories. Besides eminent writers or celebrities, fictitious names have been used; no one's real name has been revealed. A deliberate effort has been made to conceal the identity of those, whose life stories have been discussed in this book.

There is more than one reason for doing this. The first is that it seems inappropriate for me to invade someone's privacy or reveal their name, especially because I can't reach out to every one of them to seek their consent. Secondly, some close family members are discussed here as well, and I do not feel comfortable with the idea of making them a character of a book.

One more thing: there's Chinese saying that means "don't defame your own home when you are away from it". That made me contemplate the whole idea of this book for a while.

I am a big fan of Chinese wisdom and I always like reading their quotes, but this particular one made me pause and think twice.

How wide is the concept of *home*? Does it strictly mean home? Or one's city of origin? Or one's country? Or even the whole planet where we live? Or the universe? Not clear, right?

As I have been taught, when things are not clear, we interpret them in the light of our conscience, and this is how I interpreted this saying:

When God created this world, He didn't draw lines anywhere. He didn't make maps or borders. It was *our* doing that made borders, boundaries, defence forces, armies etc.

So why shouldn't I treat this planet as my home?

Why should I stop myself from saying something just because borders exist in this world *now*? Or because I am on *this* side of the border and not on the other? How would that be right?

If there's something wrong going on in Brazil I can say it's wrong. If the same thing happens in Pakistan, should I not say so, just because I was born there? That doesn't sound right to me. Surely that should be an even stronger reason for me to speak up. Besides, wrong is wrong regardless and right is right regardless. What do borders have to do with it?

The topic relates to "woman" and she lives in all parts of this planet, doesn't she?

Just like epidemics, evil norms have the potential to cause harm beyond the borders and are highly contagious in a very similar way. They can travel from one person to another, one country to another.

So, I should feel okay if I say something about my *home* while living in the *home*, with the intention of highlighting it.

"The truth will set you free, but first it will piss you off."

– Gloria Steinem

"The birth of children often goes hand in hand with the death of parents."

– Georg Wilhelm Friedrich Hegel

"Since, we all lived in the womb of our mothers we were nourished and protected by the fonua (womb) This makes us connected to and inseparable from it, and indeed the whole family of creation. If she is hurt or disrespected it affects every one of her children."

– Tau'alofa Anga'aelangi
(From Tonga Islands)

Part One

—————————————

A STORY

"Once upon a time, there was a little girl. She was only four years old. She had no brother or sister, her parents were very busy. Mummy had a university to go to and Daddy had work to do, so he could make money for the family. That little girl had to spend lots and lots of time at other people's houses, or with babysitters. She felt sad and alone sometimes.

You know who that girl was? It was me. I know how it feels when parents get too busy. But they need to be busy sometimes."

I heard my nine-year-old daughter telling this story to another kid, trying to console her because she was feeling lonely. She didn't know that I was listening. I felt a deep pang of guilt within me.

That is not the kind of story I wanted my daughter to own. No parent would.

I tried to avoid that happening, but I could not. Was it too much to ask for?

Chapter One

GOING TO MAKKAH

A friend of mine went to Saudi Arabia. This is a place where Muslims go for Hajj and Umrah, as it has the Holy City of Makkah; the most sacred and cherished place for Muslims from all over the world.

Those who can afford to go, go there, and those who can't afford to go keep longing to go there one day. That's how significant that city is.

Soon after my friend reached Saudi Arabia, all of her friends and relatives, all of them, started asking her, "Have you been to Makkah yet? You are so close now, you should really go. You shouldn't waste a minute, it's a great opportunity that God has given you. It's there right in front of you, why don't you just take it? It would not be expensive."

She was receiving these kinds of messages and reminders almost every day.

Now, this friend of mine is a really good-hearted person and a practising Muslim. She called me one day about all this and said, "I really don't like how people keep pushing me about this, I only want to go there when I really *want* to go there, not because I'm living close by or it is cheaper to go now or that people keep asking for it, or for any other reason that's just not good enough. My *longing* should take me there, not the social pressure. It's a big thing, Sara, and the reason has to be big too."

I get that, because that's exactly how I felt about being a mother.

Motherhood is a hero's journey; I wanted to be that hero only if I *wanted* to be … not for societal pressure, lack of choice or for any other reason that's not good enough, big enough.

I wanted to be that hero with all my heart in it, and *only* if my heart was in it.

If the willingness is missing, the whole gist of heroship is gone. For this very reason, I have been rating myself as an *improper mother*.

Chapter Two

VENT IT OUT

I still do not know where to start, how to organise my thoughts. Nevertheless, I have decided to open up and speak up about this.

By *this,* I mean the "Mother" side of me – how I became a mother and how I have coped with childbirth in a country where I was a migrant. What were the circumstances around me throughout this period of ten years? Ten hefty years ... yes, I have been in this role of mother for ten years now.

The way I have felt and experienced motherhood is probably very different from how people usually feel about it. Despite being a mother for so many years, I have not been able to connect and bond with this role. Consequently, I could not really connect with other mothers around me either.

It was this sense of loneliness that has finally prompted me to pen it down – *"vent it out"* would be the right way to put it.

If a person has been working in a particular profession for a period of ten years, then they will be considered somewhat senior. They are usually offered a better position, increased salary, sabbatical leave or such. The point I am trying to make is that this work of ten years, therefore, should surely give me some entitlement to speak about it.

Chapter Three

APPALACHIAN TRAIL

To me, motherhood is not a full-time job, but rather a 24/7/365 non-stop endless journey. It is a path you can choose to take, but once chosen there is no way back. There are no detours, short cuts or easier ways to go around. It is like the famed bear hunt – you can't go over it … you can't go under it … *you have to go through it.*

It is challenging and exhausting like a mountain hike, similar to the Appalachian Trail, one of the longest and hardest hiking tracks in the world. The only difference between the two is that motherhood does not come with warning signs, caution notes and measures to take.

Mothers are usually *not* told about the risks, challenges and ordeals that they might have to face on their path to motherhood (certainly not in our culture). In many cases, young women are simply *tricked* into motherhood. Every possible effort is made to hide anything that might give a young woman even the slightest insight into this whole idea. They are not advised to think it through.

The journey usually begins with these slogans: "Welcome to motherhood", "Be grateful that you are going to be mother", "You are so lucky", "Some people don't have children at all", "Some didn't have them until after many years of their married life", "I knew you would be an early mother", "Congratulations", "It will *not* be hard", "It's not a big deal, don't even think much about it", "Only few months are tough in the beginning, then you will be fine", "When the baby comes, you will forget all the pain" … blah blah blah blah.

The statement that I felt particularly betrayed by is, "It takes only one year to raise a child". I mean, *seriously?*

<hr>

Chapter Four

PROPAGANDA

*I*t appears that the whole of society, with its vigour and zest, is busy doing some sort of unpaid propaganda, preparing the women of coming generations to become mothers. There is no one to prepare your mind, to caution you, to guide you through, to support you in the upcoming jerks and jolts of motherhood. The journey is to be travelled by a naïve, unprepared, unsupported, would-be mother *alone*. And she is *bound* to be happy about this, or else she is *ungrateful*.

By now you might have guessed where I am coming from, and how my context is different from many mothers. I am not saying that motherhood is not important or that it is not sacred, or that nobody should think of going down this path. Motherhood is in fact the most sacred role that a human can play. A mother is in fact a miniature version of the Divinity of God. That is probably why it is commonly said "God loves you seventy times more than a mother". Motherhood is a path of being selfless and invisible.

Once a woman becomes a mother, she should see this as an extreme priority in her life. She is raising a human, she is bringing up a life, she is nurturing a baby, meal by meal, day by day, into childhood and then into adulthood.

We all know now that a well-raised, well-bred human can change the destiny and fate of the whole world. In fact, this is my point. When a young woman is going to take up this important role, shouldn't she be prepared? Shouldn't she be well informed? Shouldn't she be well equipped? Shouldn't she be aware of what is coming? Shouldn't she be able to make an informed choice? Isn't it the responsibility of society to produce well aware and well-prepared mothers?

Chapter Five

LIE AND LIE ALOUD

*I*n order to swim in a five-foot-deep pool, we purchase special kinds of clothes, goggles, a swimming hat, we get ourselves trained and we start swimming in less deep water before we move into the deeper pool. We do a lot of practice, and only once we are fully prepared and fear-free do we let ourselves swim in open waters. It's the same for driving cars and trucks, boating, skiing, hiking and so on.

From light hobbies to serious professions like teachers, nurses, doctors, psychologists, lawyers, scientists, accountants, architects, technicians and so on, every single profession requires knowledge, experience and qualifications. Not only that, personal inclinations, choices, willingness and aptitude count too. *Consent* matters. Even after obtaining full qualifications and sufficient experience, some professionals choose to leave their professions.

In some cases, people change profession because they realise that their aptitude was not in alignment with the profession they chose. They make an informed decision to leave their profession; a conscious decision not to take the path because they are not *willing* to. Fair and square, right?

Shouldn't the same rules apply to a woman when it comes to her motherhood choices?

It appears that society chooses to be cautious with almost every single decision of the world. But when it comes to the serious and sacred role of motherhood, an entirely opposite approach is taken.

In some cases, women are pushed into motherhood blindfolded; deliberately kept in the dark. In other cases, they are told fanciful lies; a woman is told she should be thankful if she gets to be a mum.

I once took journalism as an optional subject, and while reading through the different forms of journalism, I came across the concept of yellow journalism. One of the formal traits of yellow journalism is *"tell the lie so repeatedly and loudly that it starts feeling like the truth"*. Society's approach to motherhood appears to me to be very much like yellow journalism. The well-fabricated, well-decorated, sugar-coated lies are spoken so loudly and so frequently that one feels that they must be true, and there remains no room for doubt.

Part Two

Chapter Six

CULTURAL CONTEXT

*B*efore going into detail about how I landed on this unknown and strange planet of motherhood, let me introduce myself. My name is Sara and I was born in the small city of Sargodha, which is located in Punjab, Pakistan.

Pakistan is a society woven tightly with the threads of traditions, cultural norms, values and a blend of religion. Interestingly, social norms have an even stronger hold in this country than religion. For instance, one can easily get away with skipping prayers or zakat, but it is extremely unusual for a girl's parents to initiate marriage proceedings, as this is against norms and not inconsistent with religion.

I find this interesting, as Pakistan is an Islamic republic and the only country in the world that was created in the name of religion. Theoretically, religion should have a stronger role to play in society and the day to day lives of people, but it does not. Social norms rule society.

Pakistan is a society where marriages are arranged, people live in joint families (mostly), elders in the families have a stronghold and final say on the time of marriage and on many other matters of life, such as choosing a course of study, choosing a career, even choosing the number of kids one should have, buying a property, moving house, moving overseas, etc.

At the time when a marriage proposal is under consideration, the would-be bride and groom are expected to say "Yes" (unconditionally) to whatever option is being decided for them. And in most cases they do. As I said earlier, norms are the *boss* of the society and one needs an immense amount of courage to stand against them. Some daring individuals do say "No", but that bears consequences … unpleasant consequences.

The funny part is that marriage has problems; every single marriage in the world does. Man and woman have universal compatibility issues. The ones who say *Yes* in our culture, they keep blaming their parents for those *problems* and enjoy a blame-free life. *It was your choice,* is their mantra.

And those who say *No* and choose someone for themselves, they have no shoulder to cry on and no one to blame for these *problems.* They get frowned upon by their parents for the rest of their lives. *We told you so,* is what they always hear.

Another significant trait of our society is *shame.* Many important life issues are not discussed, merely because they fall under the realm of *shame.* Topics like childbirth, contraception, menstrual cycles, domestic violence, stalking or workplace harassment and many other feminine issues are not discussed merely because it is a matter of shame to speak up on them. They are too *private*, too *womanly* to be talked about. I feel this is a source of misery for millions of people.

Lifestyle is, however, different in villages from that of cities. Life in villages is more cohesive and connected; not only do people live in joint families, but all the people in a village are somehow bonded to one another. Norms are taken far more seriously here, and deviation from established social norms is an even bigger offence.

One's lifestyle, life choices and important decisions are closely observed by the whole little community in a village. Choices have to conform to a general set of norms. Deviations can attract serious penal actions, ranging from boycott to expulsion from the village. (This is a general and very short commentary on the social structure of a Pakistani village, exceptions do exist.)

In cities, despite the norms, young people sometimes find a way to sneak out and have some rebellion. The concepts of women's empowerment, equal rights, equal opportunities and marriage by choice are also becoming known in some educated circles in Pakistani cities. Although most of these concepts are not fully estab-lished, some segments of society such as social activists, writers, authors and lawyers, are actively working on these ideas.

Chapter Seven

GOOD CHILD

So, this is the sort of society where I was born and raised. I was right in the middle of five siblings, with one elder brother and an elder sister and one younger brother and a younger sister.

I was, and I still am, a scared person. Fear has always been the predominant characteristic of my personality. I can be scared by a car horn, someone calling my name, a ringing phone, the sound of a doorbell, the sound of wind and even the beep of a washing machine or microwave oven.

As a child I used to confess to things I had never done, simply because I was afraid of getting in trouble for not admitting them.

I remember once, when I was only seven, our parents were not home one day and we were left under the care of my elder brother, who we call *Bhai*. We were all playing in the backyard and he accidentally hit something on my head and it started to bleed. Even though my head was bleeding and I was in pain, my only worry at that time was making sure that Bhai didn't get in trouble for that, or else he would be angry at me later on. As soon as our parents came home and noticed my condition, I started saying repeatedly, "Bhai didn't hit me, he didn't" before they even asked anything.

That incident became a lifetime joke in our family. My siblings still tease me, saying "Bhai didn't hit me", making fun of my cowardice.

I was one of those children to whom parents refer as their "good child". I now feel that *good child* was also the product of this fear.

I wonder sometimes, does this *tag* of being *good* come first or the *goodness* itself?

I feel that these *tags* play a very significant role in shaping our personalities, and hence shaping our lives. We strive to live up to those tags that have been chosen for us by others.

Chapter Eight

"YES"

My family was relatively modern, given the normal and prevalent conservative standards. My sisters and I were all allowed to get an education, go to university, drive a car and work. I did my law-graduation (a bold profession for a woman) from a decent university and then I began struggling to make my career, doing internships.

It was then that my parents decided to arrange my marriage. I was told that my marriage had been fixed with a *boy* who was two years younger than me. He was living in a village and was jobless – in fact he was a student then.

That news was disturbing indeed, every single aspect of it. Women tend to seek a sense of shelter and protection in their marriage, especially women raised in a society like ours. They look for a male who will be there for them, like a caring father. I could see that I wouldn't be getting any of that from a boy who was younger than me and who was busy doing his graduation. Then there was financial insecurity. Thirdly, living in a village?

I was raised in a relatively open and free environment. I could study, move around and pursue my life goals. The thought of living in a village was suffocating.

I could see that my marriage would need a lot of *work* in order to *work*, not only on the emotional side of the marriage and the compatibility issues, but also a real-life struggle of survival, job search and finding a sustainable livelihood.

Being the *good child,* I said *Yes.* It was a difficult decision but I made it. I knew that I'd been sitting on my parents' *to do list* for a bit too long. I knew that I was an educated girl (finding a match for an educated lady is a huge challenge for the parents in our society). I also knew that my father had been diagnosed with a terminal sickness, and my "Yes" would take a huge burden off his shoulders. And it did. I remember Daddy thanked me several times for saying *yes,* as if I had done him a favour.

Daddy had been friends with my father-in-law since his youth. My in-laws were educated and civilised people. In addition, Daddy thought he would apply for a visa for a developed country for myself and my would-be husband. That way we could work on our careers overseas and I would not have to put up with the social-suffocation of the village or joblessness.

His plan wasn't a bad one, and he was taking all possible measures to keep me safe and happy. But still, there were uncertainties. Would I actually get the visa? Would we be able to get settled overseas? What if I got pregnant straight away; that wouldn't leave me any time or energy to tackle the battle of a difficult marriage.

Chapter Nine

THE CHALLENGE

With all these fears and concerns, I was wedded and I came to my in-laws' family home in the village. Now what? What do I do to make it work? The first thing that crossed my mind was to avoid pregnancy, so that I could tackle my incompatible marriage and livelihood issues first. Having a baby at that time was a *luxury* that my life could not afford.

Could I seek anyone's help on the *birth control* issue that I was facing as a newly wedded wife, living in a village? The answer was "No". No *ifs* or *buts*; a plain No.

Would my own family help? No way. Remember that mantra of being grateful for the first child *regardless*.

I was now living in the village where the hold of norms was far stronger than in the cities. There was no room to breathe for a rebel like myself. My in-laws were nice, they treated me with respect, I always acknowledge that. However, respect is one thing and breaking the norms is another. So, it was a challenge that I was facing, and I was facing it alone.

My husband was my only hope. I managed to persuade him to take me to a family planning clinic while we were on the Northern areas trip just after the wedding. It was a measure to keep my plan a secret from the family. No one would have allowed it.

Now I was sitting in a birth control clinic as a newly wedded bride with a lady doctor who was questioning me, judging me, scrutinising me for me wanting to avoid pregnancy. It was as if I was asking her for something illegal. I don't remember the exact words, but the conversation between us went somewhat like this:

Me: "I got married recently, I don't want to fall pregnant straight away, can you prescribe some medicine that will help me avoid it?"

Doctor (coldly): "And why do you want to avoid it?"

Me: "I have travel plans and also some study coming up. I don't think I will be able to manage all that with a newborn baby in my life."

Doctor: "It is not a very wise move to postpone first pregnancy, it may have some side effects. Are you aware of that?" Her tone was very bossy.

Me: "Like what side effects?"

Doctor: "It may cause hormone imbalance, weight loss or gain, and may even have some impact on your fertility in the future."

Me: "Alright, I get that, I am prepared for these risks and I still want to avoid it, can you please suggest something?"

Doctor: "Do you have someone with you? Someone *older*? (That question enraged me. I was a married woman, of legal age, and she wanted to see an *elder* with me.)

Me: "I have my husband with me, and it's our mutual decision." I tried to sound calm.

Doctor: "Look, *girl*, you don't understand the seriousness of this. I can't be part of this, if you are so serious about it, go get something from a shop."

Something? from a *shop?* What kind of suggestion was that? I was there to get advice from a qualified doctor for safe birth control options, and she was referring me to a *shopkeeper?*

And the way she used the word *girl*. I knew she took me as an indecent girl. I did not like that, but I would have happily swallowed the insult if she had agreed to help me, which she did not.

She was not acting as a *doctor* during that exchange, she was a mere mouthpiece of the society who would not approve of birth control straight after marriage. Without my permission, she assumed the responsibility of being my *elder*. I felt angry, frustrated and helpless.

Now when I look back at that incident after having two kids, I wonder what side effects she was talking about. Most of them are experienced by women *anyway*, with or without children, with or without birth control.

Weight loss? I lost a massive amount of weight after child-birth, many of my friends did too. Many women rather look forward to it.

Weight gain? Look around you. Many women battle obesity after having a child.

Fertility? This can be affected by childbirth itself, or a complicated pregnancy, a miscarriage or numerous types of medicine. Why hold up birth control as the sole killer of fertility? How is that sane? And even if it was a risk, it was for *me* to decide which risk I wanted to take; the risk of falling pregnant or the risk of losing fertility. It wasn't *her* call.

Hormone imbalance? Tell me about it. I had massive imbalance of hormones after each delivery, many women do. Postnatal depression is common after having a baby.

She did not have one solid medical excuse to say no to me, but she said no anyway.

Nevertheless, I took her advice. I went to a *shop* and bought *whatever* they could give me to avoid pregnancy.

Chapter Ten

PREGNANT

That *whatever* didn't work. I was pregnant within three months of my marriage. I can still feel the pain of those words, in those circumstances. At a small clinic near my in-laws' family home, my pregnancy was confirmed when a nurse announced cheerfully, "You are pregnant".

A lady once told me that after a traumatic car accident, she remained in a coma for a few days. When she woke up there was a crowd of medical staff in her hospital room. Before she could gauge anything, one of them moved closer to her, gathered his courage and said, "You are paralysed now … the impact of the accident has damaged your spinal cord … there is a nice wheelchair arranged for you …" He kept talking and talking, but she could hear nothing past the first sentence that he had uttered.

There were people in that room around me, talking joyfully, expressing good wishes, offering their congratulations, but I could hear nothing beyond those three words: "you are pregnant".

My heart was sinking to a bottomless well of pain. The most painful part was that I could not cry. There was no shoulder to cry on, not a single one.

I wonder, was I seriously alone? Am I seriously alone? Was there or is there any other woman who would have felt the same way about pregnancy? Was there anyone who I could open up to?

That news was followed by the usual rants of "you are lucky", "I knew you would be an early mother", "It is good news, my child", "It's a matter of a few months only", and the most horrible lie, "It only takes a year …" blah blah blah blah. I could not buy a single one of them. Not a single one of them could convince me into happiness.

Chapter Eleven

HOW COULD THEY NOT SEE IT?

Who did I end up blaming? I needed someone to blame, we all do. I picked my husband. He was nearby and an easy target for me to vent my frustration. I felt that he was responsible for my pregnancy. My marriage felt like a cage in which I was imprisoned, with the chain of pregnancy tied to my feet. I was sulking most of the time, and he turned cold in response. There were walls of silence in our marriage.

Now when I look back, I see that he was not that guilty, or maybe not guilty at all. He tried to cooperate. In fact, he was the only one who understood my context, and who secretly attempted to seek family planning advice for me. It was the societal norms, the stronghold of my in-laws and, more specifically, my family and all my female relatives. They could all see, they knew my marriage was difficult, they could all witness my struggles, couldn't they? Maybe they could not.

One of the norms of our society is to feel lucky and blessed when you fall pregnant straight after marriage. Another norm is not to seek birth control straight after marriage. The latter one is a big sin.

When we view something through a particular set of beliefs, we respond according to the way our belief system directs us to feel. When strictly vegan people see us eating meat, they feel disgust, even though for us eating meat is as normal as eating carrots or apples. It is the belief system that makes us look at things in a certain way. So the people around me probably could not have a clue as to what agony I was going through. Maybe they all genuinely believed that I was lucky, and that I should have been grateful.

Chapter Twelve

BE HAPPY

Generally speaking, I was a norm-abiding person. In fact, in my circle of friends, cousins and family, I was known for living in perfectly smooth harmony with the norms. But this one norm, I could never approve of or digest.

In a society where parents arrange marriages, they check and examine every aspect of would-be in-laws. In some cases a girl's parents literally spy on a boy's lifestyle, his character, habits, reputation, his circle of friends and his family. How can they not think through this important aspect of their daughter's future life? How can they ignore pregnancy against all the odds?

Before marriage, girls are taught how to tackle settlement and adjustment problems in a new environment. They are taught cooking and cleaning, they are told to be flexible and respectful to elders, they are taught so many other aspects, but not a single word is uttered on how to control childbirth, if needed. What if one or both of the spouses are not ready for a baby yet? What if one of them is jobless? What if both of them are jobless, or both are working and a baby cannot fit into their priorities straight away? What if the spouses are not compatible and they need to work out their issues first? What if they have no certain means of living and they cannot provide for baby's needs? How come all of this is not talked through, not thought through? How can the parents be so thoughtless about such an important aspect of their child's life?

I deserved to be guided and informed. I should have been offered guidelines and support to make a free and informed decision about motherhood. I could have chosen stronger and safer contraception for myself.

I strongly feel that I was tricked into motherhood without my willingness or any preparation, and then the whole world expected me to be *happy*.

Chapter Thirteen

WE WOULD RATHER DIE

Whenever I tried to express how I felt about having a baby, I was told not to be thankless. One famous cliché was repeated several times: "When a child comes, ways are paved for him by God." Honestly, this one statement infuriates me. We bring *God* to play his role in our lack of planning. And interestingly, we mainly do it in this area of childbirth and pregnancy.

All other aspects of life are pre-planned, organised, scheduled and cautioned. We make dams to avoid floods, we make rules and roads to avoid accidents, we give pre-emptive injections to avoid diseases, we even make rules for sports. We schedule air traffic to avoid any chance of collision. We don't say things will happen and then God will pave the way. We use our God-given *brains* to keep ourselves safe.

But when it comes to having babies, we throw everything on God's shoulders instead of using our brains to plan ahead. And the result is that in Pakistan, every 37 minutes a woman dies in the process of delivering a child for whom *God* was supposed to pave the way. Do you call the way *paved* for a baby whose mother died right after or during his birth? I can't.

As I mentioned earlier, this area of our life is governed by *shame* and *norms*. We would rather die than plan.

We don't let our babies die of deadly diseases since we are not living in a primitive age and we have access to effective vaccination. But we do let our daughters die of unplanned, thoughtless pregnancies, even though we don't live in a primitive age and we do have access to safe contraceptive options. What a system!

Chapter Fourteen

PRENATAL DEPRESSION

After discovering my pregnancy, I was depressed, but I could only be sad when alone. After realising that I had no audience I stopped expressing anything. In front of my in-laws I had to adopt the persona of a "grateful pregnant mother". Deep down I knew that whatever I was going through on an emotional level was not good.

One of the major causes of suicide worldwide is the sense of being alone in pain. The thought that *no one understands me* drives many people to take their lives. All the ingredients were present. This deep prenatal depression could very well lead to anxiety, panic attacks and suicidal tendency, complicated pregnancy and even to a risky childbirth.

In the midst of all this emotional and psychological upheaval, our visa for Australia got approved. It was big news. Was I happy at this news? Yes, I was. I was relieved to think that I could be more alone, I could be myself more and I would be able to cry whenever I needed to. I was also glad to think we would be able to work on our careers and make a living.

At the same time, I was worried about leaving my daddy behind, who was battling with cancer and growing weaker day by day. I was scared that I might not be able to see him again. I was also worried that I would have too much to care for as a migrant new mother. I had to study, as we had been granted a study visa. I had to look after home and domestic chores, find some work and ultimately adjust to having a newborn in that busy routine. With all these mixed feelings, my husband and I arrived in Australia in July 2009.

Part Three

Chapter Fifteen

CHILDBIRTH

I began my life in Australia as a migrant in an individualistic society, where norms have no real role to play, which was good. However, in Australia everyone is responsible for their own chores. Childbirth is *not* a team effort here, as it is in Pakistan.

Soon after arriving here, me and my husband both found jobs, and I started to juggle work, study and home duties. Did our relationship improve after coming here? Not really. I was still resentful, and there was a rift between us. However, we were not left with a lot of time to argue or fight.

My pregnancy was progressing day by day, week by week. I started attending doctors, nurses and the hospital. I would secretly pray for a miscarriage. By that time, I had another voice within me, the voice of a mother, who would never let me think of suicide, abortion or deliberately harming my baby. All I could do was pray for a miscarriage, so that I would not have to care for a baby in that busy life, nor carry the guilt of harming the baby either. As I am writing these lines, I find myself wondering, "Will anyone really relate to all this?"

As the delivery drew closer, another hope emerged. "I might die in the process of delivering the child." With that thought an argument would begin between "Me" and "Mother" in me:

Me: "It will be great if I die."

Mother: "You would leave a motherless baby behind, what about her?"

Me: "What if we both die? That way no one will have to worry about the baby, right."

Mother: "And what about your husband, what will he do without you?" She knew her argument was weak already.

Me: "What about him? He is grown up, he is young, he can marry again, there won't be any problem with him. He is the last person I want to worry about right now." There was anger in my tone.

Mother: "What about your parents? Won't they be devastated by your death?"

Me: "They have four other children, they'll be fine after a while. Besides, it's because of their lack of advice that I am facing this."

Mother: "But they didn't do it on purpose, they couldn't see that coming."

Me: "Really? Couldn't they? How couldn't they? You know what … just shut up and leave me alone."

40

Nothing happened. I didn't die, the miscarriage didn't happen and I delivered a healthy baby girl, who I named Mona. The childbirth was normal, but I needed a lot of stitches afterwards.

I found it difficult to stand or walk. I stayed in hospital for five days. In the daytime when visitors would come to see the baby and bring gifts, I would pretend to be happy and normal, but the moment they left I would lie there like the living dead on the hospital bed next to Mona's cot. I didn't welcome her to this world. I didn't celebrate her birth, I coped with it … I survived it.

Those sinister thoughts of wishing death on my baby, not celebrating her birth, not giving her warm hugs on the day of her birth and weeping intensely beside her cot all planted the seeds of deep-rooted guilt within me. Now I was dealing with both pain and guilt, and that tree of guilt kept growing.

I had always believed that we should not do things half-heartedly, and now I was playing the most sacred role of being a mother with *no heart*. I was nurturing a particle of the universe with no desire to do so.

One night, during my hospital stay, a nurse came to my room and announced, "I'll be on call tonight." That phrase *on call* was a bit confusing for me. I thought she meant she would be over the phone, but why would she announce that?

What she actually meant was that she would be available for us to call her. The following ten years brought home the meaning of being *on call*. And they used to say, *it takes one year to raise a child*.

Chapter Sixteen

UNIVERSE IN MY HANDS

I dreaded going home from the hospital. The thought of taking care of a newborn baby without any nurse, helpers, grandparents, uncles or aunts scared the hell out of me. The hospital staff trained me as much as they could during my hospital stay. They taught me how to clean the baby, bathe her, change her and feed her.

On the fifth day, I came home with the baby. It felt like I have been given the *universe* to take care of. I did not know where to start. Whenever my baby would cry, I would offer breast milk. But it started happening too frequently, and for too long. I remember sitting in my bedroom feeding the baby for hours and hours. I would hold the need to go to the toilet. I would remain hungry for long periods of time. My husband used to work in a bread factory and would often bring bread home from work. Many times, that bread was the only meal I could offer myself. I found it very difficult to stand for more

than a few minutes, due to the stitches, so cooking was
not possible.

Chapter Seventeen

TAKE CARE, DEAR

I was regularly receiving calls from my female relatives in Pakistan. They would say to me:

"Take care, dear."

"Keep warm."

"Initial days after childbirth are very important."

"Eat lots of healthy food, don't forget you have an extra mouth to feed."

"Have plenty of soups every day."

I would assure everybody that I was taking extra care of myself, eating more than usual and resting as much as possible. At times, while giving these assurances, my tummy would rumble with hunger and tears would roll down my cheeks.

Every day I would expect that my husband would come home and do something for me – cook some meals, or give me a little break. He, on the other hand, would expect me to welcome him and serve him a fresh meal. Both our hopes would shatter and the rift between us grew wider and wider with every passing day.

Lack of frequent meals, lack of fluids and constant breastfeeding drained my body and I ended up with terribly painful constipation, which ripped my stitches.

In the midst of all this, semester began. Barely the second week after giving birth, I was back at college for my classes. My college was close to Redfern station, in Sydney. Those who know Redfern station will know that extremely fast wind blows between the streets next to the station.

Whenever I passed through that wind tunnel I literally used to feel the need to hold onto something so that wind wouldn't blow my skinny body away. I would walk down those windy streets with the echo of *take extra care, remain warm and cosy* in my mind.

No one paved the way … it was me against the cold wind, alone.

Chapter Eighteen

WOUNDED

I would complain to my husband that he was not taking care of me at the time I needed him the most. He would complain in return that I was not there for him when he was tired or hungry. I felt wounded by his lack of care.

Now when I look back, things appear different. He told me that he was raised with servants around him. He had been served meals in bed almost all his life. He would walk to the bus stop with a servant carrying his bag.

During his stay in the boarding house, he had appointed a servant to bring food to his room and take the dirty dishes away, so he would not have to walk up to the hostel mess. All his life, he saw women or servants taking care of men. This was the first time in his life that he was doing a job without servants, and he was not being served by his own wife. How could he understand my context? How could he realise that a woman can also need care? And how could I make him realise? The concept was alien to him. I, on the other hand, was wounded, exhausted and hurt.

Chapter Nineteen

DADDY

My baby was only a few months old when I was told that my daddy's days were numbered. My sister had once mentioned that he missed me and spoke about me often. At that point in my life, I wanted to leave everything behind and be with him. I discussed the idea of going back to Pakistan with my husband, but he cautioned me that travelling internationally with a newborn was not a good idea, that it wouldn't be easy for me. Leaving the baby behind was not an option either, as I was breastfeeding. I felt imprisoned once again; chained to the baby while my father was taking his last breaths.

I had a massive fight with my husband on one of those days. I screamed at him. Why did he make me pregnant? Why did he enchain me? I used the most abusive and rough language I possibly could. It was one of the fiercest fights that I ever had with my husband, and echoes of it remained between us for months afterwards.

Daddy passed away … I became numb. I could feel nothing. I don't remember shedding a single tear over his death.

رونے والوں سے کہو ان کا بھی رونا رو لیں
جن کو مجبوریِ حالات نے رونے نہ دیا

تجھ سے مل کر ہمیں رونا تھا بہت رونا تھا
تنگیِ وقتِ ملاقات نے رونے نہ دیا

Tell the ones who weep to weep also on behalf of those
The cruel constraints of whose circumstances kept them
from weeping
We had meant to weep, weep a lot, upon meeting you
But the brevity of our meeting kept us from weeping

Sudarshan Faakir (poet)

Chapter Twenty

MOTHER TOOK CHARGE

A nurse used to visit me, to see how I was coping with childbirth-related issues and the baby. She gave me a questionnaire one day and asked me to respond honestly to all the questions in it. My answers revealed that I had a strong suicidal tendency. She booked me in to see some a social worker and I started attending regular sessions.

Those sessions were like a small window for me to breathe some fresh air and vent out my suffocated thoughts and feelings. I started liking Australia, for it offered me a platform to be myself. The social worker did not judge me at all, which was very comforting.

I can't remember the timeline of events or vivid details, but I do know that I started feeling better physically. I started taking small shifts at work and began cooking meals for family regularly. I started having more *Mother* moments, when I would feel connected to my baby. I started referring to her as *Mona* instead of *baby*. I would find it satisfying to bathe her, massage her, dress her up and do her hair.

As a wife, however, I was robotic, duty bound, and emotionally dead. I would perform all the jobs of a wife but I had no heart in it. In front of friends and family, at social gatherings, I would adopt my usual persona of *grateful mother* and *happily married woman*.

I can't say for sure, but I believe I was successful in maintaining that persona for years.

No one could peek behind that mask except my younger sister, who was and is my soulmate. She can sense my silence, she knows the meaning of my pauses over the phone. She knew when I was actually smiling and when I was merely pretending.

She came to visit us in Australia when Mona was around 10 months old. She knew straight away that I was *coping* with life, but not living it. I remember sitting beside her once at Circular Quay beside my favourite water view. I did not open up to her –I had stopped doing that ages ago – but we did talk about daddy. She encouraged me to cry, and I did. I kept crying for a long time. Soon, it started to rain. I felt that God did not want the whole world to see my tears.

Once I was fully recovered from my stitches and pelvic floor issues, the first thing I did was to find the most reliable contraceptive option and have that implanted in me. An act of rebellion by the *good child*, it gave me a sense of freedom and empowerment. I pledged in my heart never to try for another baby, no matter what.

I started taking Mona to playgroups, mother's groups and other community events, and began meeting and interacting with other mums from different countries and nationalities. I became very attentive about her immunisation, her weight and other health issues.

I would feed her, take her to parks, buy her toys, read her books and sing lullabies to her. She was becoming part of my life. The mother in me was taking over.

Chapter Twenty-One

TWO BANKS OF A RIVER

Those times were filled with warmth and love. Maybe it was in those moments that I started thinking about my husband. He was obviously present in my life, in the house, but nowhere in my heart or mind. We were like the banks of a river, existing parallel to one another but never meeting.

I started noticing his presence, and began to see his side. The spoon-fed child was now working very hard to adapt to the Australian lifestyle. He was a good employee, he was managing all financial aspects of our household, he would mow the lawn, get the car washed, do the vacuuming. Despite being raised and bred in the typical norms of a village, he never complained about not having a baby boy, he never asked for more children. He supported my decision to use contraception and, most of all, he had put up with a resentful wife for a long time now.

Although I was feeling a bit sorry for him, I still did not have the energy to walk up to him. I was depleted by the constant juggle of domestic chores, Mona, work and university. I was surely not as bitter as I had been in the first few years of our marriage, but I was exhausted and drained.

Part Four

Chapter Twenty-Two

HIBA

hen Mona was about four years old, and the toughest subjects of my degree were over, I started feeling relief. Around the same time, Mona started noticing that almost all the kids her age around her had a sibling or two. Sometimes she would play with other kids and their siblings and then tell me, "I want a baby in my own house."

When she was born, I had not welcomed her, and that act towards my daughter, a human soul, was a constant burden on my soul.

I started having open and honest conversations with my husband. In fact, we both opened up. We cried for all those tough times we had faced as a newly married couple. We offered heartfelt apologies for being rough and cold to each other, we confessed our mistakes, we explained our contexts to each other and we both genuinely acknowledged one another's contribution to our common struggle to achieve a settled life in Australia.

And for the first time, I discovered that I was not alone in the guilt I was living with; he had the same guilt too. We both felt that providing a sibling for Mona might be an opportunity for us to subside our guilt.

The mother side of me was fully convinced about the idea of having another baby, but *Me* was still shaky, scared and paranoid. "What about the pledge? What if I get depressed again?" *Me* protested.

"You are choosing to have a baby this time, not being forced. It should not make you depressed and it will make Mona happy, remember?" Mother rested her case by saying that.

Mother's arguments were stronger this time, and *I* surrendered. I got the contraception removed and fell pregnant soon after.

Interestingly, despite the warnings of the doctor who refused to prescribe contraception, *nothing* happened to my fertility even though I took the strongest possible contraception.

Chapter Twenty-Three

TRIGGER

This time, I was well informed and experienced. I knew about the challenge that lay ahead, and I was willing and prepared. The pregnancy, however, was not very smooth. I had nasty long spells of chesty coughs every now and then, varicose veins and bad asthma attacks.

I was still studying, as I had a few practical components of my degree to cover. I kept working on my assignments until around the eighth month of the pregnancy, when it became difficult to keep my laptop in front of me, then I decided to take a break from study.

Childbirth went smoothly, and I was blessed with another baby girl, Hiba.

Did I just write *"blessed"*? I am actually surprised at how the *Mother* in me persuaded me to accept a baby as a blessing. *Hiba* means "gift"; I named her as such.

I can't remember for sure what triggered it, but I was a victim of post-natal (postpartum) depression again. I had fits of boiling rage. I would throw things hard on the floor to show my anger, hit my head against hard objects, and I would cry and even scream when alone. I would think about killing myself, and once again I found myself hating everyone around me, including my two children.

Apparently, things were a lot more supportive compared to my previous childbirth. I had a warm and well-heated room that my husband had set up for me to stay in with the baby. I was not skipping meals. I did not have to go to the wind-tunnel of Redfern, and I had a network of support around me.

But I was sad, angry and fearful all at the same time. There were times when the thought of being alone in the bathroom would terrify me.

When I discussed my situation with my nurse and local doctor, they explained that my feelings were due to the hormonal imbalance that women experience after child-birth – many women experience extreme behaviours and find it difficult to maintain equilibrium.

I knew this must be true, for it was coming from profes-sionals, but something inside me was telling me that it was a *trigger*; painful memories of my previous childbirth had come back, and they knocked me down again.

I read this in a book about maternity-related depression and found it to be true:

"No woman is absolutely immune to postpartum blues. Perhaps the strongest and most confident among us are the

ones who are, in fact, the most vulnerable. Interestingly, this psychological roller-coaster can happen just as easily with the second, the third or even sixth pregnancy as with the first."
Excerpt from Elif Shafak's book *Black Milk*.

Chapter Twenty-Four

INSTITUTIONALISED

I started seeing a psychologist regularly. During therapy, she told me to be *kind* to myself. Kind to *myself?* That was a very new and strange idea for me. The thought had never crossed my mind before. I always thought kindness was for *others.* It would be selfish to be kind to oneself.

She asked me to watch myself closely and note the actual moments when I became unkind to myself or didn't give any consideration to myself. I started watching myself, both present and past conduct, and it turned out this was how I was treating myself and responding to my tiny little wishes:

- Feel like eating chocolate? No, an apple is better.
- Want a cup of coffee? Milk would be good.
- Want to watch a movie? No, go do the dishes in the kitchen.
- Want to read a nice book? You have an assignment coming up, go and work on that.

- Feel like buying a colourful scarf for myself?
  How about socks for Mona, she needs a new pair.
- Want to sit in the sun? The floor isn't very clean,
  you'd better clean that.
- Want a fresh meal? There are leftovers to be
  finished.
- Want to cook fresh? There are things in the
  freezer, use them first.

The list goes on and on. In short, I had stopped considering myself as an entity – if anything, I was a mere *afterthought*. My life had become all about goals. Goal to eat healthy for the sake of the baby … Goal to pass each subject … Goal to achieve a high enough score in each exam, each assignment to make it through … Goal to score required bands in English test … Goal to raise healthy kids … Goal to develop healthy eating habits in kids by setting a good example … Goal to keep running household smoothly … Goal to make enough points for visa … Goal to support the family financially.

The goal to consider *myself* could not fit anywhere in that jam-packed goal-oriented life of mine.

I once read that if someone lives in certain tough life conditions for a long time his body and mind get attuned to it, and when he is removed from those conditions, he finds it difficult to enjoy the normal and comfortable life. This phenomenon is called "institutionalisation" and this behaviour is referred to as institutionalised behaviour. It is commonly observed in people who serve long sentences in jail or in correctional centres. They lose the ability to relish their freedom, once free.

After spending seven long years in a constant rush, I had lost the ability to act normal or to take life lightly. I was now being told to take a pause and be *kind* to myself. I had no clue where to start.

Part Five

Chapter Twenty-Five

MATTER OF SORROW

After Hiba's birth, my husband and I started receiving calls and messages from our relatives in Pakistan. They were apparently saying "Congratulations", but their well-wishes were coated with *ifs* and *buts*. I don't remember all of them, but some of the comments went somewhat like these:

"Congratulations … but I wish you had a boy this time."

"I am happy for you … it would have been great to have a son this time though."

"Your family would have been complete if it was a son."

"Girls are great too, but I wish you had both."

"Don't lose heart, it will be a son next time, I have faith in my prayers."

"You should try for another one."

"One more chance would not harm."

Someone even said "What can be done? It was the will of God."

I am the kind of person who would disagree with norms in more subtle ways; would never dare to open up or speak up. I never had, and I still don't have, the guts to do so.

It was my husband who took charge of this task. He told them off in a clear, loud and blunt way. He even had heated debates with some of them. I was a proud wife; his response to those misogynistic remarks against his daughters made me proud. He was there for me, he was there for them. The *boy* that I had married now appeared as a *man* to me.

I once had to call a previous employer of my mine, who I had worked for in Pakistan, for a work reference letter.

He took my call and kindly agreed to provide the letter. While I was on the phone with him, he heard my kids making noise in the background.

"How many kids have you got?" he asked.

"Two girls," I said boldly, which was unusual for me. I often say "two kids" and try to divert the conversation to some other topic, especially in front of people from whom I expect sympathetic remarks.

There was a long pause, then after recovering from the shock, he said, "Don't worry, God will give you a son as well."

I felt like screaming at him "NO ONE IS WORRIED HERE; WILL YOU EVER STOP?", or hanging up on him, but I instead said "keep praying" in my usual submissive manner.

Remember the norms that I mentioned earlier? This is another norm that most Pakistanis and many Southeast Asian people live with.

"Not having son is a matter of sorrow."

Chapter Twenty-Six

CLIP THEIR WINGS

I have made several attempts to understand what makes people want to have *sons* so desperately. I have asked this question of many people, and this is what I have been told:

"Son will support the parents one day."

"Daughter will go away, son will remain with the parents."

"Son is protector and saviour of the family, daughters are weak, what can they do?"

"Son will lead the family."

"Family's name depends on the son, he will take the name of his father across the generations."

"Having a son determines the worthiness of a woman."

"What can sisters do without brothers?"

"Even prophets asked for sons from God … it's noble to wish for sons, you know, sort of religious." And so on.

In the social structure that I grew up in, many of these statements are true … but not necessarily *right*. This is how I feel about them:

There is no guarantee that your son will grow into a responsible and good man.

There is no assurance that he will live with you.

There is no guarantee that he would want to support you.

There is no guarantee that he will become sufficiently financially independent to support you, or himself even. He may start depending on you instead. (I have personally and closely observed many cases like that. All the drug users I know are boys.)

He may never bother about looking after his sisters, parents or anybody else for that matter.

And no prophet of God ever said that it is an *obligation* to ask for or wish for a son. Stop manipulating things.

He may choose not to marry. He may not have children or a son, and consequently the family's name will be gone after another generation. Then what?

And by the way, why does one need to bother about his *name* after he is gone? What benefit will that bring to the departed soul? This is literally beyond me.

If someone really cares about his name that much, I would suggest to him, "Go and do something worthwhile and your name will stay here forever. Don't wait for a *son* to get this job done for you." Noah's (AS) name stayed, his son's did not, remember?

The point is, when you can't see the future, how can you make having a son a condition for you to be happy? Be happy with what God has chosen for you. Have faith in Him, for "WHEN A DAUGHTER COMES, GOD PAVES THE WAYS."

No amount of human struggle can determine the gender of an unborn baby, it is purely and solely in the hands of God.

Be happy when God gives you a daughter; stop treating her arrival as a matter of sorrow.

Stop determining the worth of a daughter by what she gives birth to. **Respect her anyway.**

Do not make a woman give birth to three or four or seven or nine girls in an attempt to bring you a son.

What do you think happens to those girls who are brought into this world while endeavouring to produce a boy? And what do you think happens to children who see that their brother's birth was celebrated and their sister's wasn't?

I can tell you the answer: they grow up knowing that they were *not* welcome, they were *never* looked forward to, and they were *never* wanted.

Their self-esteem is stripped by their own parents and relatives, in their own homes.

They live the life of second-rate citizens in their own country on their own homeland.

Worse, if they happen to have a brother, he will receive love, attention, care, better food, better clothing, education, opportunities for a better life, right in front of those sisters. You know how that feels?

It hurts. And it never stops hurting.

In short, you clip the wings of our daughters and then complain that they can't fly. You snatch away all the possible opportunities from them to grow into strong and self-reliant citizens of society and then say "they are just *girls* and they are *weak*".

What you are doing, in effect, is producing millions and millions of unhappy people. You are creating an unhappy and ungrateful society. Just look around and you will see it everywhere.

I used to wonder how a woman could possibly force another woman to go through the same pattern of life that she had endured, force her to have several children for the sake of wanting a boy, or make them feel worthless for being a woman or for bringing women.

Turns out, happiness and self-esteem, like so many other commodities in life, can't be passed on if you don't have them … Hence, the chain of misery continues.

ایک ہی روش ہے یہ
ایک ہی خلش ہے یہ
ایک ہی سمندر کا
ایک سا کنارہ ہے
ایک خواب ہے جس کی
کرچیاں بکھرتی ہیں
اک رات ہے جس میں
سسکیاں ابھرتی ہیں

ایک ہی ڈگر پہ یہ
ایک جیسے لوگوں نے
ایک ایک کر کے کیوں
روشنی مٹا دی ہے
تیرگی بچھا دی ہے
ایک ہی زمین ہے یہ
ایک ہی خدا اس کا
ایک ہی تو سورج ہے
ایک آسمان اس کا
ایک سا ہے دل سب کا
ایک سی ہی روحیں ہیں
پھر بھی درد بڑھتا ہے
پھر بھی آہ تنہا ہے
پھر بھی عشق رسوا ہے
ایک جیسے لوگوں میں
ایک جیسی روحوں میں

Its oneness everywhere ("Fair is foul and foul is fair[1]")
The One takes shapes everywhere
Be it way or unease
Be it borders of the seas
Be it dreams fallen down
Be it sobbings haunting town
People of my caste do bleed
Why this hatred why this greed
The only way is dark and bound
By the blood of shiny crown
O ye earth! To thee we belong
Thou art source of thought and song
Be it sun or its God
Be it soul or its heart
Oneness prevails yet one is afall
Odes are at mourn and love is trawl
Toll is high for every sigh
To thee I owe my rainbowed sky
Yet dreams are chained and wings are torn
Wilt there be an end to tame less storm!

Chapter Twenty-Seven

BRAINWASHING

Someone said to me once, "it's the woman herself who wants the son, no matter how many pregnancies she will have to go through. Nobody *makes* her want that."

Oh yes, she does, I agree.

Let me tell you how it all begins; with a girl who has spent her entire childhood listening to these kinds of rants:

"You are so lucky, you have brothers."

"You are so unlucky, you don't have a brother."

"Pray from God to give you a brother."

"So and so's aunty has seven sons, she is so blessed."

"They were four sisters and had one brother only."

"So and so's cousin has three girls only, poor thing."

"So and so's aunty got divorced because she could bring no son."

"So and so's uncle remarried because his first wife was having girls only."

"So and so's family is celebrating the birth of their son, he is born after six sisters, they are all so happy."

"Neighbour sent sweets, they just got a son born to them."

And as she grows a bit older, she would listen to these mantras:

"I pray you have as many sons as you wish for." (This has been said to me several times in my life.)

"I had five girls then a boy, I hope this would not happen to you."

"I am going to Makkah and I will especially pray for you to have a son."

"Please ask for a son for me, I have heard that the very first prayer in Makkah is never denied."

"That girl was so lucky, she had her son in the first year of her marriage."

"I am so happy for you; your first child is a boy."

"You have a son first then the rest goes all smooth."

"You will settle down in your marriage easily if you have a son."

What else do you think she is going to *wish* for, after listening to all this? When she knows that all her worth, her place in the house of her in-laws, her marriage, her happiness, everything is so heavily dependent on having a *son*, what else do you think she would want from life?

This is how she is *made* to wish for a son.

Do you know what this process is called? Brainwashing.

This process of brainwashing is not new, and is not restricted to any particular region of the world.

Simone de Beauvoir, a French author from the last century, in her book *The Second Sex* (1949) "argued that women were at a disadvantage in a society where they grew up under 'a multiplicity of incompatible myths' about women. Instead of being encouraged to dream their own dreams and pursue meaningful projects for their lives, Beauvoir argued that the 'myths' proposed to women, whether in literature or history, science or psychoanalysis, encouraged them to believe that to be a woman was to be for others — and especially for men. Throughout childhood, girls were fed a steady diet of stories that led them to believe that to succeed as a woman was to succeed at love — and that to succeed at other things would make them less lovable."

(An extract from an article by Kate Kirkpatrick, published on *The Week*.)

The only difference is that over time, things got better in some countries for women, but on our side of the world they remained the same.

If you are doing this brainwashing or have been doing it, please stop.

If you have been watching it happen around you, please discourage it, and if you have become a victim of this trap and you have no power to fight it then all I can say is that my heart feels for you and I pray for you.

But if you have the power to change it and you still choose to do *nothing*, then you are guilty of it.

Let me give you a little tip here before I move on: happiness is a flower that grows from the seed of gratitude. Plant that seed within you. Once you are happy, you are luckier than the rest of the crowd anyway. It's not rocket science.

Chapter Twenty-Eight

MERE CHANCE

I am often told to "take another *chance*, it may be a boy this time".

In other words, I should bring a human soul into this world as a *chance*. And what if it's a girl? What will she be then? A *missed chance*.

Daughter = *Missed Chance*

Bringing a unit of the universe into this world as a mere chance is a *sin* in my humble dictionary, and I would never dare to commit this sin.

Every soul should be welcomed and celebrated, for it is a tiny particle of eternal divinity.

For heaven's sake, stop treating your daughter as mere *chance.*

I once failed to welcome my daughter, and waves of guilt still hit me for that *sin.*

There was once a Prophet (Mohammad PBUH) who would stand up in honour of his daughter, spread his shawl on the floor for her to step on. Wasn't that to teach us how to treat a daughter? How to welcome her?

Sick of all the unhappy responses I received after the birth of Hiba, I broke the silence and wrote this on one of my social media accounts:

"As I am experiencing full-time motherhood this time. This is how I feel; I feel that I owe hundreds of apologies and thanks to my mother. I feel that a woman does not remain human when she becomes a mother, she becomes superhuman. I mean can a man clean the kid's poop right in the middle of his meal? And that too for days and days and years and years. I am sure it's disgustingly unimaginable for men. I don't mean to demean men through this writing, so I won't linger on this point anymore. Man is playing his role quite well and he is acknowledged and thanked for that … I come back to my point again that woman is a marvel as a mother. She is a babysitter, nanny, a nurse, a doctor, a psychologist, an entertainer, a playmate, a cook, a groomer, a cleaner, a round the clock guardian and a legal parent (mostly) as well.

She is sacrificing her rest and entertainment. She is having broken meals and broken sleep. She has interrupted phone calls and fussy drives. She's even on call when she is in the bathroom or toilet. She is hanging clothes on the line and her own clothes are being pulled by little hands. She is cleaning the floor and crumbs are being spread around the next moment. She is feeding the baby and gets a spray of baby food on her face with a little sneeze. She is changing the diaper and gets a fresh spurt of pee near her mouth. And all of this goes for days and days, weeks and weeks and year by year ... if anything, it changes the form only. In many cases women's life and health is at stake in the whole process of childbirth.

She is giving all of these services for free; no charge at all. She is even adding the love and compassion on top of it.

And yet, as a society (Asian societies in particular) we do not celebrate the birth of a woman as we do of a man. May God forgive this lack of gratitude. May God help us mend our ways."

Chapter Twenty-Nine

THE TIP OF THE ICEBERG

*L*et me take you to a few memories here, to show how welcome our daughters are.

I was once standing at a bus stop, waiting for the bus, while in Pakistan. I noticed a family standing there as well, a father, mother, three daughters and a son. The kids were all under 10 years of age. I could tell by their clothing that they were not rich people.

A juice seller approached the family and I saw the father buy a pack of juice and give it to the boy, while the girls were watching it all. My heart sank with pain. I knew it was poverty but I also knew that it was not just poverty … it was a reflection of our ugly social behaviour towards our daughters.

~

I remember this incident from my childhood …

My family once went to a party at one of Daddy's friends' places (who we used to call uncle).

Uncle had organised this party to celebrate the birth of his son. This son was born after four daughters.

We had not been to their house for a while. My mother noticed another girl child in the house and asked uncle in surprise, "Last time we were here, you had three daughters; how come you didn't share the news of the fourth daughter?"

Uncle laughed and said, "Was that news worth sharing? We thought it wasn't."

Even as a child, I did not like that gesture.

On another occasion, an elderly female relative of mine told me that when she gave birth to her fifth daughter (she had that many girls in order to get another son), people came to her house for "*afsos*".

For those who don't know, *afsos* is a formal expression of grief on someone's death.

This is how ugly things have been. This is how ugly they still are for millions and millions of women out there.

I am not an authority on religion, but this is what I know for sure:

"When any of them is told about the birth of a female his face turns dark, and he is filled with suppressed anger." (Al Quran - 16:58).

Now, I know this verse has some contextual background, but one thing is certain: this is how God is describing a trait of the people he does not approve of.

Part Six

Chapter Thirty

NOWHERE

As I started recovering from postnatal depression and other childbirth-related issues after Hiba's birth, I resumed my studies. I started working on all the assignments and presentations that needed to be done.

I was then required to take an English language test in order to score enough points to lodge my Permanent Resident Application. It took me three attempts, but thankfully I got there.

Hiba was almost one year old when we were finally ready to lodge the application as a family. It was my seventh year in Australia by then. In all those years, I had not been able to visit Pakistan even once. I kept working towards my goal to settle in Australia, nonstop, like a blind horse.

After seven long years of rigorous work and with no smell of my homeland, I was exhausted, really really exhausted.

As a child and teenager, I used to read stories of travellers and about people who would go and settle in other countries. I read many times that one feels sad and lonely on foreign lands.

What I didn't know then was that one gets so lost in the struggle of settlement that it becomes hard to recognise one's own self. All the windows to yourself close, one by one, until only visas and dollars are left to be worried about. You remain nowhere. I was nowhere. I was not like myself in any way; the calm personality that I used to carry was gone. The sense of humour I'd had during my university days was nowhere … reading, writing, poetry … everything had flown away in the hurricane that I was in. My looks had also changed … it was the face of a pale, exhausted person that I now saw in the mirror.

Chapter Thirty-One

SETTLED

We finally lodged the permanent visa application (PR) and then visited Pakistan. It was naturally an overwhelming experience, but I won't go into much detail about that, as it is not relevant to the scope of this book.

During our stay in Pakistan, our PR application was approved and we finally became permanent residents of Australia. A big milestone in life was achieved. We came back and began our life as settled Australians by the grace of God.

Chapter Thirty-Two

SAND IN THE WATER

As I mentioned earlier, I felt different about the whole idea of being a mother. I felt that I could never become *one* with the *mother* in me. Throughout the thick and thin of the last ten years, I had managed to maintain the *Me*. There were days when *Me* would become silent and dormant, but there were days when *Me* was clear and alive.

The mothers around me are *one* with motherhood, like the way sugar dissolves in water completely …. there is no *Me* left in them, no separate identity.

I'm more like sand in water … no matter how hard I try, I don't get dissolved – the colour and texture of the sand can still be seen in the water. My mother used to say "When a baby is born, woman dies and only mother is left." It just didn't happen to me.

Chapter Thirty-Three

SMALL-TALK SURVEY

I can't say for sure whether it was the desire to find someone like-minded or just the curiosity to understand the perspective of other mothers (*willing mothers*), but whenever I was surrounded by mums in playgroups, at mother's groups, in parks, at doctors and even on social occasions, I would always find myself asking certain questions, such as:

How many kids do you have?

How many did you want?

Were all pregnancies planned?

Did you always want children?

What makes you wish for children at all?

Was it scary to have the unplanned one? How did you cope?

Being in a multicultural society like Australia gave me the opportunity to meet and talk to women from almost all parts of the world. So the data that I collected is quite rich in cultural diversity. It also spans a period of 10 years, starting from 2009.

The responses that I have collected so far are as follows:

"I have two, and yes I always wanted children."

"Yes, I was surprised by the unplanned pregnancy, but not panicked, of course."

"All of my pregnancies were planned, and I have three children so far."

"I have one, it was an accident … but a beautiful one." I remember she laughed as she said this. She was from the Tonga Islands.

"I have two, but I really wish I could have more."

"I always wanted children … I wish I could have one at least …" This was said to me by Shu Lee with tearful eyes; a dear friend of mine from China, who could no longer have children due to her profound disability.

"I wanted to have a soccer team of my own kids, but I stopped at two. It's exhausting, I realised." A lady from a European background said this.

"I wanted five but now I realise it'll be difficult, so I may go for three."

"What else would you do with your life, if you don't have kids?"

"Having a life is a privilege that nature has given us, and giving birth to children is a way of showing gratitude for that privilege; life is a gift and I would like to pass it on."

That came from a very dear friend of mine who is of Indian background.

"At least one of them will be good enough to look after me." This hilarious comment came from a Lebanese woman who had 11 children.

"I didn't have children for years, then after several treatments, God gave me two."

"I had to have IVF in order to have the baby, got only one." An English lady told me that.

"I wanted to have children in my twenties but my husband did not agree … and now I am 35 and it's my first pregnancy" An Australian woman said this regretfully for having such a late pregnancy.

"My children are the world to me."

"Some women prefer a career to children, I reckon it's a selfish approach." An Australian-born Asian lady said this to me.

"Babies are cute, I just can't resist the idea of having them."

"Not having kids feels selfish to me and I think it is selfish." This was from an Australian workmate of mine.

"A woman without children is like a tree with no leaves." This is from my mother.

"Life is like a barren land without kids, and you know I always wanted children." This came from my younger sister.

"I had to risk my life to have my son, and it's worth it." This came from a disabled lady (white Australian) with a serious spinal injury, whose disability got worse after having the baby. She took the chance of pregnancy despite the knowledge of all the risks it carried.

This list goes on and on … All of these responses have been making me feel small, ungrateful and of course alone.

Chapter Thirty-Four

WHO IS SELFISH HERE?

There is, however, another set of responses which is worth mentioning here. They go along these lines:

"You know when you don't have children in the first year or two of marriage, people start asking questions."

"You should not be late in your first pregnancy at least; you may take chances with the second."

"It does help giving a shut-up call to people."

"Children determine the worthiness of a woman, especially sons."

These and other similar responses all came from people of my own culture or from some Indian women that I met.

Now, these are the responses that make me feel that my approach wasn't altogether wrong, and that I am probably better than those who would bring babies into the world as a mere shield to protect them from social pressure. What they *actually* want is armour against society, not a child. How is that *not* selfish?

What *I* always believed is that one should bring a human soul into this world when they are ready, free and willing to welcome him/her – a welcome that a newly born soul duly deserves. And how is that selfish? If anything, it sounds more *responsible* to me.

Chapter Thirty-Five

EAST AND WEST

What I found interesting was that motherhood is such a global phenomenon. The thought process of a mother remains the same in the developed and western countries like Europe and Australia, and in the Southeast Asian, Arab or non-Western side of the world.

If a woman chose to remain childless and pursue other life goals, she would invariably be labelled selfish and judged in all cultures. I found this extremely surprising.

The difference, however, is that in the Western world, a woman is at liberty to make choices. She can use any contraception she likes, she can have a late pregnancy, a long gap between pregnancies or no gap, or even no pregnancy at all. Whether those choices are then approved by society remains a separate debate.

It works the other way around on our side of the world: a choice has to be approved first and then taken. I find this not only suffocating, but also a violation of a woman's right to make a decision about a matter that will impact her life far more than it will anyone else in the world.

Before moving on, let's see what our religion has to say about it. I am quoting Susan Carland here (I know, her name sounds too Aussie, but trust me she is a Muslim). Susan is the director of the Bachelor of Global Studies at Monash University, and the author of *Fighting Hislam: Women, Faith and Sexism*. This is how she sheds light on the rights of woman in Islam, in her book:

"Classical Islamic law affords women the same right and obligation to an education as it does to a male, the right to financial independence (in both earning and spending, including owning property, entering contractual agreements and initiating enterprise), the right to keep her name after marriage, the right to sexual satisfaction from her spouse, the option to use contraception if she desires, the right to divorce, the right to initiate and refuse marriage, the right to be a religious authority equivalent to men, the right to social and political participation, and the right to financial maintenance from her husband – as well as viewing her as a spiritual equal to men. It even states that a woman is not required to serve her husband food or clean his house."

In case you are wondering, there are numerous reasons for quoting Susan Carland, but these are the most relevant ones:

Despite being raised in a Christian family and in the Western side of the world, where Susan had all the reasons to hate Islam and follow the stereotypes like many others, she chose to investigate and then chose to be a Muslim. I am not quoting her because she chose *Islam*, I am quoting her because she *chose* Islam and she is not Muslim because she was born as such.

When we do things *willingly*, we do them a hell of a lot better. That's the whole point of this book, by the way. That's why I am quoting Susan.

Secondly, I wanted to avoid the possibility of bias as much as I could, and I could not think of anyone else who would be able to comment on women's rights in Islam in this contemporary world, free of cultural bias, norm bias or shame bias. Admittingly, there is still the risk of gender bias and religion bias, to which Susan herself responded with these words:

"Clearly, I am approaching the topic as an insider. I am a Muslim woman researching the experiences of Muslim women. No doubt there's some bias to that, but it's an illusion to think outsiders don't have biases of their own."

The third reason comes from the fact that she not only embraced Islam, she also went on to do an enormous amount of research on Islam – so much so that she ended up doing her PhD thesis on the topic of Muslim women fighting sexism at different times and in different parts of the world.

Being a student of Law and of Islamic Law, I always had confusion and questions bubbling up in my mind around this aspect of Islam, namely how Islam genuinely treats women.

When, for instance, I attended a lecture on the topic of marriage in Islam and learnt that marriage is a legally binding contract, just like any other commercial contract comprising of *free* consent of two sane *adult* parties, offer and acceptance, consideration, witnesses and so on … I could not help questioning how such a balanced religion, which sees woman as *adult* as man, as *sane* as man and as *free* as man, can then back the mass mistreatment of women that I see around me in a Muslim society?

It was Susan's thorough research, involving interviews of scholarly Muslim women from different parts of the world, that confirmed that I am not alone – there have been Muslim women at all times and in all parts of the world raising similar questions and fighting against the patriarchal version of Islam to which Susan referred as Hislam (*his* Islam). Her research further confirms that the solution lies in the true interpretation of Islam, as she quoted from one of her participants, Zafreen:

"Islam and its teachings are capable of giving women an equal footing in society to men, and that Islam does not relegate women to the private sphere. I really believe some Muslims have distorted our teachings and forgotten our heritage. I believe that Islam can be used as a source of empowerment for women. I believe that. I don't need to rely on Germaine Greer or a secular model in order to reclaim my dignity as a woman. Islam can give me that."

Excerpt from Susan Carland's book *Fighting Hislam*.

The fourth reason stems from the Paris attack in November 2015. After that sad incident, Susan started receiving loads of tweets full of hatred and bullying, telling her "*you love terror – you love war – you love oppressing women – couldn't you just be an atheist?*" and so on. In response, she tweeted that she would donate one dollar to UNICEF per hate tweet she received – an act that won the hearts of many, including mine. In other words, she chose the approach "you throw rubbish at me and I will do good in return".

You throw rubbish at me and I will do good in return … ring a bell? Wasn't that exactly what was demonstrated by our Prophet Mohammad (PBUH)?

That is why I chose this one Muslim lady to shed light on women's rights in Islam.

Part Seven

Chapter Thirty-Six

WHAT'S THE BIG DEAL HERE?

I survived, right? My fears and concerns about childbirth didn't actually come true. I managed to come out of that societal pressure. The pregnancy did not kill me. I had two kids safe and sound. I survived two horribly scary bouts of postnatal and prenatal depression. I did not actually kill myself, despite the fact that I thought about it several times. No one was harmed. My marriage survived, too.

So what's the big deal? People have unplanned pregnancies all the time, in all parts of the world. So what? What damage is it causing at the end of the day? Why am I fussing so much about this one little aspect of women's life?

Let me tell you a few stories that might answer these questions.

Before I do that, let's be clear here: it is not unplanned pregnancies that I am talking about, it is the *tricked* pregnancies, it is the *blindfolded* pregnancies and the *forced* pregnancies.

Now let's go to the stories.

Chapter Thirty-Seven

MARYAM

After coming to Australia, the first and only Pakistani class fellow that I met in my college was an intelligent girl from the northern areas of Pakistan. Let's call her Maryam.

Maryam was very kind and supportive, although very quiet. She guided me a lot on the college rules and time tables, etc. After being with her in a few classes, I noticed that she would vary rarely smile, and she would only talk when she really had to.

I asked her if everything was okay in her life, and this is what she told me:

"I have a few months old daughter, who is not with me. I had to leave her overseas with her grandparents ..." She burst into tears.

"I did not want to come here without her ... it's her breastfeeding stage ... but my in-laws forced me to take this decision or else they would make their son divorce me," she continued.

She told me that when she lodged her visa application, her daughter was not yet born, so she could not be part of the application. The visa was granted to both parents but not to the newborn baby. Her in-laws wanted her and her husband to jump at the opportunity, so they forced her to go to Australia without the baby.

It was almost two years before Maryam's daughter could join her here in Australia.

An infant separated from her mother in the years she needed her the most. Do you see the *damage*?

Contraception could have saved that from happening, couldn't it? Planning ahead would have helped to avoid this. But that, of course, was out of the question.

After a little while, I met an Indian woman with the same story, having also been forced to leave a newborn behind. And then another and then another … all from our side of the world. All emerging from blindfolded pregnancies.

What stories would all those children own, I wonder …

Chapter Thirty-Eight

SIMA

Sima appeared to be barely 20 years old. I met her a few times at our cultural events here in Sydney, but never had a chance to have a detailed chat with her. Sima had a 10 month old baby girl.

When I met her for the last time, she sat next to me. After saying hello, I came to my usual point, and asked her:

"Were you planning for the baby, when you conceived her?"

"No, actually not," she replied. "I came to Australia just after getting married and had the baby straight after. I didn't think that I will fall pregnant this quick, it just happened." She made a failed attempt to smile as she said that.

"Did you cope okay with the childbirth then?" I asked.

She did not reply, her face sad. After a long pause, she managed to say:

"We even had to pay for hospital cost of childbirth, with our current visa status."

Something triggered in me … I could not say a word after that.

This was my shortest survey.

Chapter Thirty-Nine

ZENAB

This story is somewhat similar to my own. Zenab came to Australia in similar circumstances to me. She came with her husband and they both wanted to settle here, but were struggling.

The couple didn't have a child until two years after their arrival here. Zenab's husband, Ali, was against the idea of having children while they were struggling (God love him). But Zenab persuaded him that they should go for pregnancy no matter how hard the situation was, and he reluctantly agreed.

Their first child was a girl, who is 8 now. After the birth, Zenab faced many health issues, including postpartum depression, panic attacks and suicidal tendencies. She also had to study in the midst of all this. One can imagine how much attention and care her daughter would have received under those circumstances.

I met Zenab only once while she was in that situation. When I met her again many years later, I learnt that they had another child (a boy this time). Her second pregnancy and childbirth had been full of complications too. She told me that her daughter didn't start solids until the age of four, and her son had speaking problems. Both the children were suffering from serious vitamin deficiencies and taking many supplements at this young age (her son was only 3). Her daughter had recently been diagnosed with depression, at the age of 8.

"You were in Australia, you should have avoided pregnancy and saved your children from facing those hardships. You weren't that old, you could have planned babies a bit later," I commented, my heart pounding with fear for making such a comment to a Pakistani woman.

"Look Sara, we shouldn't avoid kids just because we have problems in our lives. I have seen many people regretting such decisions … and don't you know that God paves ways when a child comes …" She then repeated a whole series of clichés which I grew up listening to and have no mind to repeat here.

I knew better than to say "O yes! It's all God's fault, I remember, and how can *I* forget, He should have paved the ways … it has got nothing to do with your planning."

"It must have been hard though for you to look after kids while you have been unwell yourself?" I dared to ask.

"No, it was fun," she said without looking into my eyes.

At the end our meeting, she did not forget to give me a friendly reminder that I am an ungrateful person and that I should reconsider my thought process.

～

These are the kind of women who I classify as perfect victims of brainwashing; a disease very common but not very easy to cure.

I understand that there are problems and diseases in this world anyway, and not all the issues relate to untimely childbirth. However, bringing your own babies into this world *knowing* that you will not have enough time, energy or resources to attend them is simply wrong. Childbirth is not an absolute virtue … it is qualified.

Chapter Forty

FARIDA

I met this lady in Pakistan two years ago; a lady of extremely humble means, with a sick husband and nine children to feed. She was a domestic worker. She was hardly 35 years old, but looked far older. Her own health was in poor condition, as evidenced by the wrinkles on her face and the circles around her eyes.

Three of her kids were working (in farms or in someone's home as domestic workers) to support their household financially. Two of them were under the age of ten.

Do you call this situation a *damage*? I do, and I do it without the slightest doubt … damage to so many human souls, simply because of a lack of contraception. Babies were coming to this family *non-stop*. Not because they were wanted or welcome, they were just happening thoughtlessly.

I couldn't help asking her, "Why did you plan so many children when you couldn't afford them?"

She scoffed, as if to say how ignorant I was.

When I insisted, she replied, "There was no one to tell me what to do about it, no one gave any contraception advice and the kids kept coming." Her voice was full of sorrow.

If I couldn't access that advice with all the education and means available to me, how could she? I thought helplessly.

Contraception is not an option ... it's not a question ... it's not something to ask for ... it doesn't even occur in people's minds, because it's a sin, a big social sin ... until the damage is done.

Farida is not an anomaly; that story is everywhere. Every third or fourth house would have a woman with similar circumstances.

Mumtaz Mufti, one of my favourite authors, once wrote, "knowledge-wise there are four types of people:

Those who know and they know that they know;

Those who know but they don't know that they know;

Those who don't know and they know that they don't know;

Those who don't know but they don't know that they don't know."

The norms in our society have brainwashed those women to the extent that they don't even *know* what they are being denied ... they don't even know *what* they don't know about their perfectly legitimate right to access contraception at the right time. Their perfectly legitimate right to say *no* to any further pregnancies or to *a* pregnancy if they can't afford it.

Chapter Forty-One

IRSHAD

*I*rshad was a young and intelligent girl who was born in a poor family. Her parents could not afford to educate her, so she ended up being a domestic worker (maid).

After being a maid for a while, she got married and found out early on that it was dangerous for her to conceive, so the doctor recommended adoption. The couple adopted a child, but her husband kept on forcing her to have a child of their own. She fell pregnant, carried the baby for 9 months and then died during childbirth.

~

Irshad used to work in the home of a Pakistani artist and illustrator named Shehzil Malik. Shehzil shared Irshad's story on her social media account in October 2019, along with these comments:

"Every time I read 'Mera Jism Meri Marzi' (meaning 'my body, my choice'), I see a comment by a man saying that these 'loose liberal women' just want to walk around naked – sometimes a bikini is mentioned – and I wonder what planet these men are from. This slogan is not about an imaginary handful of privileged women playing dress-up. This slogan is about the vast majority of women who don't have autonomy over their bodies. This slogan has as many contexts as the many, many ways women aren't given control over their bodies. This slogan is about all people – across class and gender – whose bodies are policed, shamed, violated, exploited, abused – right down to being killed.

Next time you read 'My body, my choice', I hope you also think of Irshad. Her name literally means 'Speak', so speak up for her."

I am left speechless on this …

Chapter Forty-Two

AUNTY

This story has been told to me by a friend of mine and it is the story of her maternal aunt. Let's call her Aunty for the sake of narration.

Aunty was a happily married woman living in Pakistan. Soon after her marriage, she fell pregnant and had a son. I wish I could say *then she lived happily ever after.* But that did not happen.

After a little while, she fell pregnant again, this time with a girl ... and that's where her miseries started. No one was happy with that *outcome.*

She was persuaded to take another *chance* in an attempt to get *another* son. She took it, and had a girl again – and then another and another and another.

After five girls, she was pregnant again. She was told it was a boy this time. Everyone was happy! The D day came, she went to labour ... and never came back. The baby boy survived, but she didn't.

Chapter Forty-Three

MEHNAZ

*B*efore I begin this story, let me caution you: the details are confronting.

This story was shared on Twitter by a Pakistani journalist named Diaa Hadid in November 2018. It goes like this:

Once upon a time, there was a girl named Mehnaz, who was living in the northern areas of Pakistan. She was under the age of fifteen when her parents arranged her wedding.

As one would expect, soon after her marriage, she was told by her husband to bring a *son* or else there would be consequences.

She fell pregnant and had a girl … this happened again and again and again in the pursuit of son. By the age of just 19, this poor girl had given birth to four girls.

When she fell pregnant for the fifth time, she was told by her husband that she would be thrown out of the house if she gave birth to one more girl.

Fearing that it might be a girl again, Mehnaz decided to do something that is not easy to even imagine for many ... she planned to kill her unborn baby before the delivery, by herself.

With the little knowledge that she possessed, she did every possible thing that she knew that could hurt the foetus. She took all the tablets that she could find, lifted heavy things, consumed whatever food and drink she believed would help her achieve her goal ... until the day when she felt extreme pain in her stomach. Her husband took her to the midwife, where she delivered a dead baby.

This tragic story did not come to an end there. Mehnaz had two more self-administered abortions, fearing the same *consequences*.

In the end, Mehnaz did manage to give birth to a healthy son and she did survive that exhausting and risky journey of several childbirths and three abortions.

It was pure luck that she managed to survive such a risky path. For as naïve as she was, she was making a perfect attempt to kill herself too, each time she tried to self-administer an abortion.

～

The reporter who shared this story stated something along the lines that *Law is not clear on abortion in Pakistan.* I felt a fair degree of unease with that remark. I mean, what has *law* got to do with the day-to-day life of a Pakistani?

Norm is the boss there, and *religion* comes next in the chain of hierarchy. *Law* is merely a lazy clerk sitting at reception complaining that there isn't enough stationery in the office.

When a woman gets raped in Pakistan, for instance, *law* would just say "let me see if I can find the ink to write your report", and that ink would never be found.

And if one would think of going to *religion* for help, this fellow would dutifully stand up and say "let me consult the *boss*" and then, having had a detailed meeting with the *boss* and making one wait for hours, he would come back and say "look, I understand it is painful to bear what has just happened to you but the best course is for you to stay quiet. I'm sure you understand how *shameful* it can be to bring this kind of stuff up …"

And this is how the whole machine operates. Why talk about *clear* or *unclear* law in the wake of all this? No matter how clear it might be, IT WOULD NOT MAKE ANY DIFFERENCE.

Do you think that Mehnaz's parents would have given any consideration to *law* when they arranged the marriage of their under-aged child? Or that her husband would have thought about what *law* might have to say when he was abusing his wife for not bringing a son? If your answer is "yes", then my response is "ha ha ha".

～

One can't help wondering how on earth *parents* can throw their child of such a tender age into such a cruel marriage. How is this any different from throwing one's child into an ocean full of tides, *knowing* that their child doesn't know how to swim? How could they do it? How can one be so heartless? How could they *not* think through it?

Or maybe her life wasn't worth a thought; she was a *girl*, after all.

~

The reference to religion in this story is the reference to the *Mulla* of our society who would never dare to speak against the child marriage, against domestic abuse, against rape, against acid being thrown on women. He would never discourage the blind greed for a *son* which has turned into a savagery and which is causing such misery to women of our society on a massive scale. What is wrong with you all? Why do you stand by and watch this? What is our fault? Are we not daughters of Eve (Hawwa)? Are we not a creation of God? Were you not told to be fair and just to the women?

THIS IS NOT FAIR AND THIS IS NOT JUST.

~

I am not a theologist and I don't claim to be one. But there are some questions that I can't help raising. Islam, as we know, is a religion that states that if you face oppression and violence, stand up and fight against it, if you can. And that is why there are wars in Muslim history. And then it states that if you can't fight, at least go away from the oppressor/s, and that's why we see migration (*hijrat*) in Islamic history.

Now my questions are, would these rules change if they were to be applied on a micro-level? Would that oppression become legitimate if it was being committed by a husband, for instance? Should a woman put up with it and not fight against it? Should she not at least try to alienate herself from the oppressor if needed? The safety of the Muslim community was God's concern, but is the safety of women none of His business? Is it Islamic when parents tell their daughters to keep putting up with the abuse in their domestic life?

Does this appear right to you? To me, it doesn't. The God that I understand, with my limited sensual perception, cannot be that unfair.

Chapter Forty-Four

SOFINA

In November 2017, while I was sitting in a cafe during my lunch break, I came across a heart wrenching news story about a mother killing her own daughter, in Melbourne.

How can a mother do that? To her own daughter? The child was only 15 months old. It was terribly sad. I read the whole story.

Her name was Sofina Nikat, she was a woman from a Fijian background, living in Australia, (Fiji has very similar cultural norms to those shared in India and Pakistan). She had been recently married – the marriage was arranged, and the couple had serious compatibility issues. Sofina was the victim of domestic violence and she decided to flee the home where she was living with her husband. She moved to a women's shelter.

I was still wondering, how could she?

Then I came across this line: "... family members told detectives she had spoken numerous times about killing herself and her baby, asking her daughter: *Why do you have to be born and why do you have to make my life so miserable?*"

I got my answer ...

What happened next is nothing less than shocking. The Victorian Court attached significant weight to the depressive psychosis that Sofina was suffering from and decided to reduce the charge from murder to infanticide. The difference between the two is that murder carries the maximum penalty of 25 years, whereas infanticide has a maximum penalty of 5 years. Sofina was sentenced to just a 12 months' correctional order only.

Infanticide is the act of killing one's baby under the influence of extreme psychological disturbance. Postpartum depression has been now recognised as a serious mental disorder by the American Psychiatric Association, which described the connection of this disorder and the killing as such:

"Infanticide is most often associated with postpartum psychotic episodes that are characterized by command hallucinations to kill the infant or delusions that the infant is possessed, but psychotic symptoms can also occur in severe postpartum mood episodes without such specific delusions or hallucinations."

Excerpt from *Diagnostic and Statistical Manual of Mental Disorders*: 5th Edition DSM 5.

A fiction writer from Turkey also wrote on this topic. She personified this intense depression/psychosis as *Lord Poton's uncle* and analysed it in these words:

"Psychosis (Poton's uncle): This is the most dangerous and alarming psychological transformation that a new mother can go through. Those who come into contact with Lord Poton's uncle can end up harming themselves, their children and their surroundings. It requires long-term and serious medical therapy to be rid of him."

She further states:

"It was not only the 'unhappy' or 'unfulfilled' women who suffered from postpartum depression. New mothers of every class, status, religion and temperament were susceptible to it. There were no golden formulas to explain each and every case. Yet, there were a number of causes that triggered the process, such as previous experience with depression, physical health issues during pregnancy, social problems, lack of cooperation of close relatives and friends, sudden change in the surroundings and so on."

Excerpt from: Elif Shafak's book *Black Milk*.

In light of all this, it does not appear surprising why Sofina ended up doing what she did.

The story about Sofina was aired on all main news channels Australia-wide and published in all the mainstream newspapers.

What this story confirms is that this disease is contagious, and it does cross borders.

What it also tells us is that a woman's emotional health is of *crucial importance* and it must be taken care of, otherwise she can't take care of herself or her child.

Chapter Forty-Five

FAIZA

This story is also local. Faiza was born in Pakistan and is now living in Melbourne. She got married to a very well-settled and rich Pakistani man.

After a few years of marriage, the couple moved to Australia. While packing their stuff, they also packed all the prevalent social norms there; they arrived here with heavy bags.

Their marriage was okay, they were happy. Then a son came along, and they were even happier, of course.

After a while, the husband remembered about the bag that they had brought with them. He opened up the bag and realised something was missing from their happily married life: *another son.*

He went to his wife and said, "I want another son."

His wife agreed. After a little while, she fell pregnant; irony of fate, she had a daughter. Nobody was happy. Her husband was sulking, and her in-laws were blaming Faiza for bringing a girl when they wanted a boy.

Faiza persuaded herself to fall pregnant again in an attempt to live a life of harmony. A girl came again … and then again.

After three girls, she refused to go for another pregnancy. By now her life was practically hell. She was reminded every day how pathetic and useless she was … she was repeatedly told to take another *chance* … she was even being threatened with serious consequences …

She finally succumbed to the pressure and took another chance. This time it was a boy … now everyone is happy again – things are all good apparently – but this woman is exhausted and resentful, living a life she did not choose, having gone through pregnancy after pregnancy *unwillingly*.

Do you see any reason why she is not capable of turning into another Sofina? I don't.

Do you see the damage here? That's how high the stakes are. That is what I am fussing about. **That is the big deal here.**

My story is the story of a survivor. A survivor's story can never be all good … after all, there was something to be survived, a problem or issue that needed to be addressed. I was simply lucky enough to survive it. Not everyone is that lucky and it should not be left to *luck* … we should move ahead and fix it.

I came across a few arguments from people saying "Islam can't encourage contraception because contraception equates to murder and our religion is against murder." (I seriously feel that they were mixing up the ideas of abortion and contraception.)

With all due respect, I strongly disagree with this mindset. First of all, you can't kill someone who doesn't exist in the first place. Secondly, it is the *lack* of contraception that leads to or has the potential to cause many, many murders, both emotional and physical murders, not the other way around, and *that* is what our religion opposes.

To me it sounds as ridiculous as saying to a person who doesn't want to get married, "Since you are not marrying, you are not having babies, and since you are not having babies you are basically killing them, and that is against religion."

Wow!

Part Eight

Chapter Forty-Six

CATEGORIAL DIVISION

$\mathcal{I}$ lived all my life in Pakistan, up until the age of 26, when I moved to Australia. During that period, I encountered the following two types of women (broadly speaking):

- Those who want children and have them – the acceptable kind, of course
- Those who want them but don't have them for some reason (not acceptable).

If we dig a bit further, we will come across these sub-categories:

- Those who want children and have sons; BRAVO! This species is highly credited and complimented for the *favour* they have done to the society
- Those who want children and have both girls and boys; they are acceptable too – or, to put it more

honestly, they are forgiven for having girls, as
they have compensated for their *sins*

- Those who want children and have girls only;
  they are our social sinners, who have burdened
  the family with girls. They are always persuaded
  to keep giving birth to babies until they have a
  boy or boys. Sadly enough, many of them die in
  the attempt
- Those who want children but have none; their
  existence is a question mark. They are outlawed.
  They are sometimes criticised and at times pitied
  for having to live such a *pathetic* and *useless* life
- Those who don't want children; this species does
  not exist in Pakistan, or at least I have never
  come across or heard of anyone in this category.

Chapter Forty-Seven

HIGHLY DEPLORABLE

There is one more category that I really want to talk about here: those who didn't want children, and have girls. Needless to say, this is a highly deplorable category. I am the only one who belongs to this breed, I have not found anyone else so far.

Not that everyone knows what I have been thinking or wishing all along. Had that been the case, the list of my sins would go something like this:

- I did not want children; at least not unless I was ever ready for them.
- I have girls – *two* of them; this is heinous.
- I am perfectly okay now with what God has chosen for me; neither panicked nor miserable. *Just imagine.*
- I do **not** want a boy or boys. Now this deserves some serious penalty. (I do not understand how this works. I mean, how on earth could giving birth to a baby with male organs possibly make

my life any happier or better? Seriously, how? Not understanding this whole idea would probably make it an even bigger sin.)

- I make no attempts to fall pregnant again. I take no *chance* in an effort to have a boy.
- I am content with two, a number not good enough for a woman who has *only* girls.
- When I am reminded by my elderly relatives that I am such a miserable woman for not having a son, when they express their concern for me and tell me how they pray for me to have one, I say *"thank you so much, please keep praying"* and then I laugh about it secretly.

I could never relate to women around me due to all these *flaws*. A Pakistani friend of mine, who is very well aware of this criminal history, once said to me, "Don't come back here girl! You know that you are from some *rebel clan* that does not belong here."

She was absolutely right, I do not belong there. Maybe that's why God kept me here in Australia, in a place where I enjoy perfect immunity from all the social wrongs that I am guilty of.

I am a rebel, that's true. But where is that *clan* that I belong to? That's what I have been looking for, for so long now.

Part Nine

Chapter Forty-Eight

THE REBEL CLAN

*I*n 2018, in the ninth year of my motherhood journey, a few things happened.

Someone in my suburb placed an open bookshelf in a street very close to where I live. That bookshelf had the words 'street library' written on it. I noticed it when I was taking my daughter to playgroup one day.

One could take or drop a book from the library without any rules, deadlines, membership or fines. I loved that cute little thing. I loved the whole idea, actually. I picked up a book from there one day to read on the train while I travel to and from work.

The book was *Eat Pray Love* and it was written by a famous American writer, Elizabeth Gilbert (Liz).

Why did I choose that book? I liked the cover with the picture of an actress who I like, and the reviews on the book were good, so, I thought it might be a good time killer.

This book was a turning point in the way I thought about motherhood. The writer shared her experience, inter alia, of how she kept contemplating the idea of having a child for so many years and finally decided not to have one. She described in vivid detail how she came to that decision and stuck with it. (That was only a tiny portion of that book, by the way – it went far beyond this idea.)

I enjoyed the book thoroughly, every bit of it. I was also glad to know that there is at least one woman on this planet who thought of *not* having a child. Who thought in a similar way as I once did. This is how she described her thought process:

"But did I have a responsibility to have a family? Oh, Lord, **responsibility**. That word worked on me until I worked on it, until I looked at it carefully and broke it down into the two words that make its true definition: the **ability to respond**. And what I ultimately had to respond to was the reality that every speck of my being was telling me to get out of my marriage. Somewhere inside me an early-warning system was forecasting that if I kept trying to white-knuckle my way through this storm, I would end up getting cancer. And that if I brought children into the world anyway, just because I didn't want to deal with the hassle or shame of revealing some impractical facts about myself—**this** would be an act of grievous irresponsibility."

I love this bit, of course, but what struck me most was when she wrote beautiful and spontaneous conversations with Divinity in her diary. After reading those dialogues I felt that this was not a book but a *package of love* from heaven.

This is what she taught me through those conversations. The following paragraph is not an extract from *Eat Pray Love*, it's my impression of how God would have addressed me if I were the one calling for his attention in the most miserable moments of my life:

"God loves you no matter what – if you choose to be a mother he will love you – if you choose not to be – he will still love you – if you welcome the arrival of children in your life – he will love this gesture of yours – and if you fail to do so – he will understand you – he will always be there for you – you notice his presence or not – you feel him or not – he will remain there – his love is not conditional to your choices in life … his love is far too deep, wide and generous … he or his love does not get bothered with these trivialities – so stop hating your-self – stop labelling yourself as a social sinner – stop calling yourself an improper mother – stop condemning yourself for not being able to welcome your first child … be kind and gentle to yourself – love yourself and, most importantly, forgive yourself."

In another section of *Eat Pray Love*, the author wrote a few questions in her diary addressed to Divinity, when she was knocked down by loneliness and depression. Immediately, she was able to write the responses as well, as if the Divinity spoke through her. The response went like this:

"I'm here. I love you. I don't care if you need to stay up crying all night long, I will stay with you. If you need the medication again, go ahead and take it — I will love you through that, as well. If you don't need the medication, I will love you, too. There's nothing you can ever do to lose my love. I will protect you until you die, and after your death I will still protect you. I am stronger than depression and I am braver than loneliness and nothing will ever exhaust me."

Sometimes in life, we know how things work, we know all those beautiful moral values that parents or religion have taught us, but we still get stuck – we still get lost. At those times what we need is a little help – an assurance from a loved one, a word of comfort from someone we can trust and believe, someone to say these little simple things to us which we already know.

Chapter Forty-Nine

I simply needed that little push, and Liz Gilbert provided it.

She is on my friends' list now; I don't care if she knows about me or not. She has been around me through her books for more than a year now. She has guided me, supported me, consoled me. She even scoffed and laughed at me where I was wrong, she corrected me and advised me where needed. She amused me and made me laugh several times. She drew me closer to God through her writing. She mentored me in the writing process. She did everything that a friend would do. And I relate to her in so many ways – I mean, she's a woman, she's a writer, she's a reader, she's fond of travelling, she's fond of food, she lives on the same planet as me, we are alive at the same time and of course her thoughts on motherhood are similar to mine. What else does one need to qualify as a friend?

Thank you, Liz, – and thank you God for sending her over to me through her books.

Liz was the first person I came across who belongs to what I call my *rebel clan*.

A famous Pakistani writer Mumtaz mufti once wrote the following about his close friend Ashfaq Ahmad (a well-known Pakistani intellectual): "when he talks, he doesn't actually talk, he merely hides what he doesn't want to talk about, his secrets, sadness, thoughts, emotions, reactions or simply anything that he doesn't want to show the world; he would hide that behind that *curtain* of his monologues". He actually became so good at that art that people started loving those *curtains* … he became a celebrity, famous for his beautifully presented, story-studded shows in which he would merely talk and people would listen to him in silence.

Turned out, I had been doing the same for years. When among people, I would talk about the weather, politics, schools, food, recipes, movies, plays, furniture, clothing, fashion. I would talk about anything – anything but the real *Me*.

The only difference was that I didn't become good or popular as a result of those curtains.

This happened because I knew I had no audience, no trustworthy or compassionate listener, so I hid. I hid behind those curtains in a place that was dark and lonely, and remained there for so long that I lost the ability to speak my heart out. I lost my expression.

Paulo Coelho in his world-famous book *The Alchemist* wrote a beautiful line: "And, when you want something, all the universe conspires in helping you to achieve it."

It felt that the whole universe, in its utmost generosity, set itself to help me find my *clan*.

~

Around the same time as I encountered Liz in 2018, another incident happened. It was a cold winter morning and I was on my way to work. As I walked along a busy street in the city, I heard someone shouting "excuse me" from behind me. I looked back and saw a girl running towards me with my phone in her hand.

"You dropped your phone near my shop," she said, handing it to me.

I had purchased a bottle of water from her a minute ago; I must have dropped my phone while paying her. I thanked her quickly and ran to work.

It did not occur to me that this little incident could be of any significance.

I would often stop by her shop and chat. I soon discovered that she was from Pakistan and fairly new to Australia. I felt more comfortable talking to her after I knew that. Every now and then I would go to see her during my lunch break. Soon it became a routine.

After a few meetings I began to get to know her, and found she had a combination of extremely unusual human traits.

She had the ability to *stay in the moment*; she could enjoy the present time to its fullest. This rare ability has been described by many Urdu and Punjabi Sufi poets and writers as "Saahib-e-haal", which literally means "a person who stays in the moment".

I personally found this exceptional. Most of the people I have met or known in my life have a tendency to cling onto either painful memories of the past or some fear of the future.

In my humble opinion, many of the health issues faced by humankind all over the world have their roots in our inability to stay in the moment. We humans find it very difficult to *move on* or to *shut the door behind us* or to be *carefree* of the future.

This new friend of mine, Maria, would keep marching in life, keep throwing all the heavy sacks of painful memories behind her, keep shrugging her shoulders at the future worries and keep starting each day afresh and light. I found this simply amazing.

That was not all. Maria also had a strange shock-absorbing system in her hardware somewhere. I once told her about someone I knew who had lost a newborn daughter; the baby passed away within a few hours of her birth.

Maria heard this news and fell silent for a long moment. And then (when her shock-absorbing system came into action), she said, "You know what, this world is not a very ideal place to be in. I mean, look around you, isn't it full of worries and problems, diseases, poverty, crimes, wars and so much more? That little soul got free of all this. Believe me, she is free and happy wherever she is at the moment. Don't worry too much."

I once heard that in Japan, where earthquakes are a regular event, the government was funding the construction of earthquake proof/resistant houses and buildings. That motion-absorbing technology is called oil dampers. The dampers used in the buildings are filled with thick oil. When the building shakes during an earthquake, the dampers counterbalance the shaking because the oil slides in the opposite direction, minimising the tremors. Maria was very similar to those remarkable Japanese buildings: she would stumble in response to the jerks of life, but would never collapse.

She was living alone in a new country by herself and working like a blind horse to support herself financially. There were days when her employer would bully her, abuse her, refuse to pay her wages or use racist remarks against her. There were days when she would discover she had to pay a hefty tuition fee at short notice, there were moments when she would get some painful news from her family overseas.

Even in those tough times, she was capable of saying "let's enjoy coffee at the moment, life is too short, things don't matter as much as we think they do, this planet is only a *pale blue dot* in the bigger scheme of things, what are we then? An insignificant tiniest fraction of a mere *pale blue dot* ... just chill." She would often quote this idea of a *pale blue dot*, which came from her favourite philosopher, Carl Sagan.

She was different from the usual joy-killers that we often see around us. And while this was all nice and impressive, we still weren't connected in a *friends* way; at least I wasn't, I was still behind my *curtains*, until the day when we went for a walk …

I have no memory of what we were actually talking about, but I do remember her saying this:

"You know what, I don't want to have children, once I get married, *if* I get married." She laughed, as if she was not sure about the idea of getting married at all.

I missed a few heartbeats … was this really happening? This was not someone from a book this time. **A real alive person – a woman, a Pakistani woman, from my own culture and religion – was saying *this* to me**. It was so unreal, so surprising, it felt like a dream for a moment.

"Don't you think this poor world of ours is so full of problems, there is so much hatred, racism, class difference, materialism, shallowness and so much more … I don't feel like bringing a human soul to this mess. It's so full of burden already, at least, *I* don't want to be one adding up to it … I would rather adopt an orphan and share some of the burden. What do you think?" she continued in her spontaneous, fearless style.

"Can you pinch me?" My voice came from a distant place. "I want to check if I am dreaming or not."

Then I told her: "You are right, you should not have a child if you are not up for it … besides, it's your own life, you should be in the driving seat of *your own life* at the very least."

I added "bringing a human life on earth is a big thing, and you should do that big thing only if you have big

152

enough reasons to do it … otherwise you won't be able to do justice to that cumbersome role, and it might hurt you … it might hurt others, too … so it's a big NO, if you ask me."

It was after this conversation that we became friends, and this is when I came to know that I had finally found someone who would listen to me and not judge me.

She asked me one day, "What worries you so much?"

This time I didn't hide, because I knew I could trust her. In fact, she was the only one I could trust.

I came out from behind my *curtains* and took her to a dark place within me, one I kept hidden from the whole world. For years and years, I had been storing bags full of worries, fears, guilt and shame in that hidden place …

"I haven't seen anyone who would have tried to run away from the idea of pregnancy as much as I did … who would have seen their unborn child as a heavy burden … who would have welcomed their baby the way I did … who would have wished to die because of pregnancy … who would have even wished for the death of their unborn child … who would have come across the idea of taking their own life just because they had a baby … who would have shed tears next to their newborn's cot, not tears of joy but of pain and distress … and now I worry, I fear that I'll be punished for all those horrible things and thoughts, now I worry that the law of *karma* will hit me … or it might hit my children (God forbid), or it might hit anyone around me who I love or anyone around me just because they are related to me … when other mums tell me how happy they are it makes me feel so small, so bad …"

I went on and on and on. She listened to me – she is a very good listener. Not only that, she consoled me, supported me and even appreciated me. This is what she said to me:

"We all have tough and dark moments in our lives … we all have evil thoughts cross our minds … we all want to die or want someone else dead at some stage of life … we all fail to do at times what we think we should have done … but you survived all those moments and evil thoughts without harming anyone … you didn't hurt anyone … you harmed no one at all, and let me tell you this, as it might make you feel better: you are a great mother." (Was I? Really? Wasn't I a thankless, sinful and improper mother?) "You are raising your kids in such an organised way … you have structured a beautiful household … when I go to your place I get the real homely feel in your home … so much so that I want to create a home just like yours one day."

So strange, I was never able to see myself from this angle until she pointed out all that to me … I didn't know I had all these descriptions as well. The most unbelievable bit was that I was able to inspire someone.

This is what happens to us when we are too focused on guilt or pain; our vision just becomes too blurry and too limited. We fail to notice the truths and beauties of life that are just in front of us, waiting for us to notice them.

After knowing all that, seeing all that, and acknowledging it, I actually felt a lot better.

Maria made me promise her that I would throw away all my worries and fears and that I will live a happy life. We actually ended up doing a ceremony. I wrote up all my *stinky stuff* on a piece of paper and burnt it *alive* (it feels even better to say *alive*). We then went to a favourite beach of ours and handed over the ashes to the ocean.

A cremation of miserable and lonely Me.

It was also an idea that I learnt from *Eat Pray Love;* ceremonies help us heal.

This is how close I got to the *rebel clan* ... and God knows, it was a beautiful experience.

God's love

When good things happen to me I always see it as God's way of showing his love towards me. The man who set up the street library and led me to read *Eat Pray Love* ... dropping my phone in that shop, meeting Maria – they weren't just coincidences, they were omens, signals to open up a new version and a new angle of life to me. This is what He does ... this is how He does it.

Liz Gilbert came in a subtler way, through a book, like mum's first call to the dinner table. Maria came in a clearer, louder style, to get me out of those dark places where I had been living for ages, as if to yell at me and say:

"Enough of your stupidness ... now get the hell out of there and have some life. "

I decided to listen and move on. I decided to take some action that would help me feel the change.

We all have some *special* kinds of things at home – nice clothes, delicate crockery and dishes, nice bed sheets, nice bath mats, table covers and so on, all saved up for special days, guests or going out.

I started offering all those nice things to myself. I started having tea in my favourite special cups, I started wearing nice clothes at home, I started wearing bold and bright colours. I bought myself some colourful earrings, I covered the dining table with the best cover I had, and I started buying nice grocery items (I had never done this before, I would always go for cheap). I offered tea and biscuits to myself just like we do to guests. I started offering nice and fresh meals to myself instead of just leftovers. I started doing decorative things around the house – I even decorated my bathroom with pictures and flowers.

Not only that, I joined the local library and resumed reading books. I started giving some time to myself. I took myself to my favourite water views in the city, just to see the shadow of colourful lights in the water, which is a favourite scene of mine. I went to the rivers and lakes to see the shadow of clouds in the still water. I gave myself some time to sit on the lounge, look at the trees and do nothing. I let myself laugh and cry like an alive person. I allowed myself to have some time out from the routine life without feeling bad.

All of those efforts did not go in vain … I started feeling the change.

Chapter Fifty

"O MY GOD"

Not long ago, I went to an Eid celebration party with my family. There were a lot of Pakistani parents there too. The party progressed, guests got introduced to each other and conversations began. I started asking my *usual* questions to other mums (I don't spare any opportunity). Most of the answers were the same as ever, but then something strange happened.

One of the mothers, who had just introduced us to her two cute children, a boy of 8 years and a girl of 4, told us that she developed a strange muscle and bone disease after having her first child, and doctors told her that it would not be safe for her to have another one.

"Then why did you plan for the second baby?" I could not help asking.

"My husband was very supportive, he didn't want me to have another one, but there was so much pressure from the in-laws that I could not resist it, I had to go for another one." I could see grief on her face as she talked.

"It's not that they don't care for me," she continued. "They don't even let me touch any household chores, they are nice and polite – but when it comes to having children, they are not willing to compromise, and since the second child is a girl, they are unhappy about it and are pushing now for me to try for another baby. They want two boys at least." Her eyes had flooded with tears.

"But you are in Australia now, with your husband and kids, how come they still are able to pressure you or impose their decisions on you from that far?" I asked.

"I recently moved here; both of my children were born there," she said.

"But you have moved on a permanent basis now, right?" I asked.

"Yes, I have, but that doesn't make any difference. They know how to keep influencing my life," she said helplessly.

Sadly, she was not the only case. I have met many women complaining of how their in-laws keep dictating their lives, even from overseas. I cannot understand why when a woman is seen as *adult* enough to have a baby, she isn't seen as adult enough to make the decision to have one or not.

Then I saw myself doing something I had never thought I was capable of. I stood up from the lounge where I was sitting, went over to her and said, in a very affirmative, bossy but motherly tone:

"Listen! You are not giving birth to another baby, okay? You are in a free country now, you don't have to be scared of anyone, and if you don't know how to

seek help, ask me and I will tell you what to do, where to go for contraception or any other support. I know the knack of it all."

O MY GOD … was it *Me*? Did I really just say that? Who was this bold woman? Where did that power show come from? I simply could not believe it.

The woman was stunned too; she looked at me in surprise. She might not have received such a daring piece of advice ever. But then we both laughed at what had just happened.

I then insisted that she take care of herself, as her kids need and deserve a happy, healthy mother. She seemed persuaded; I really hope she was.

But where did this *expression* come from? I was speaking my heart out – and in a Pakistani gathering! I kept wondering, I still do.

Someone up there is in a rewarding mood, I guess.

Part Ten

Chapter Fifty-One

WHEN MONA CAME

When Mona came, the Mother came too. Then this Mother was in charge, she took over … she called in Hiba too … I was left behind … there was no room for *Me* in the household … Mother had to leave *Me* behind, not because she wasn't kind enough or big-hearted enough – mother is the most kind-hearted person, we all know that– but Mother has to set her priorities. The kids were young, they needed her most. *Me* could wait. *Me* was an adult, after all, and Mother knew it … So, I waited and waited and waited, and then years later – a decade later – Mother got back to *Me* … she let *Me* in, and I was warmly welcomed, just like Hiba was welcomed.

This is what she said to me:

"I know I took very long … it must have been hard on you … I acknowledge that. I know your pain, I don't deny it. I don't deny your existence; I don't deny the existence of your pain, either. You went through a lot. I won't judge you, I won't call you ungrateful, because you are not, but here's what you need to know. A mother is a giver. She would never take away what's yours. I know I marched over, I took over, I came uninvited. I took your days away, your nights away, your years away, your peace away. I admit I did it all, but here's what I'm giving you back: enrichment, fulfilment, satisfaction, joy and bliss. You can be yourself here … I will attend on you just like I do to Mona and Hiba. You can live in this household just like Mona and Hiba … with a sense of entitlement, not with a sense of shame."

"Remember one thing," she continued. "All those years were the cocoon years … the hardest, toughest time that one needs to grow. The suffocating and tightening environment was vital to give you the colours, my dear butterfly."

It is customary in Pakistan for beggars to go from door to door asking for alms, and mothers usually give a bowl full of wheat flour or uncooked rice, from a sack which they keep filling. I was sitting on the doorstep of my own home and Mother was filling up my sack with bowls of love. She kept filling and filling and filling, and when there was no space left, she started showering me with love. I kept sitting there, my eyes flooding with tears of gratitude.

I was once a person of expression, a person of creativity, a person who could get in contact with inspiration, but I lost all that exactly ten years ago. I once read somewhere "worst missing is missing yourself". I experienced this terrible thing, and it wasn't a pleasant experience, believe me.

It was this motherhood, an exhausting, tiring journey that I kept walking on for so long – that I am still walking on – that brought everything back to me … all of it. I was left with an even better, even purer version of myself. I was given back my expression and creativity. I was also given the strength to be myself. I was given back my sense of humour, too. The debt got paid off … with a high interest rate.

Chapter Fifty-Two

A LETTER TO MY DAUGHTERS

*D*ear daughters,

Motherhood is a heavenly place to be. It is the most sacred role that a human can play, it's a job that makes you feel embellished. It is a job in which you don't get paid in cash but you do get paid in kind – that is hearty laughter, chuckling eyes, giggling sounds, warm cuddles, joyful tears and many, many more blissful moments.

It will also earn you a loving family, a sense of accomplishment, long-lasting companionship and an enormous amount of respect.

It's a journey of being invisible; if you open up the pages of history, you will find incredibly well-raised men and women, war heroes, saints and prophets, science heroes, heroes in the world of medicine and technology, saviours of humanity, all these tremendous people raised by wonderful but invisible mothers whose names are not quoted in the pages of history.

And, my children, it requires an immense amount of generosity and spirit of sacrifice. It requires you to disappear and merge into a bigger cause; the cause of nurturing the universe.

It is a journey of sleepless nights, tiring days, interrupted meals, dirty nappies, bottom rashes, nasty coughs, messy floors, loads of laundry, fussy fights, silly tantrums, doctor runs, pre and postnatal depression, daycare problems, schooling/education issues, huge, long-lasting never-ending responsibilities and much, much more.

In the pages of history, you will also find that not all the mothers were biological mothers. Some chose to be mothers of many without giving birth to a single child; the women whose names are shining in the leaves of history. Dr Ruth Pfau, Susan B Anthony, Fatima Jinnah, Clara Barton, Elizabeth Gilbert, Nannie Helen Burroughs and Helen Keller are just a few examples of women who chose to be mothers of many; they raised many, saved many and inspired many without giving birth to their own children.

In my humble opinion, the path of not being a mother isn't easy either, for it requires you to abandon the honour of being the mother of your own children.

If you choose to go for motherhood, I am with you and I will guide you through it.

If you choose not to go for it, I will support you and guide you through this too.

Be truthful to yourself, my dear daughters, and please be kind to yourself, too.

Lots of love and prayers,

Your Mama.

Chapter Fifty-Three

MOTHERLAND

"*I*s it a girl or boy?" An Australian woman once asked me this when I was pregnant with Hiba. She knew I had a girl already.

"It's a girl," I replied.

"So, you will have two girls! That's beautiful" She had a big joyful smile on her face when she said that.

I feel grateful to Australia for giving me a society like *this*, where I am welcome and so are my girls. Where having a girl is simply *beautiful*. Where I can roam around with my girls with pride. Where I am not seen as a pathetic being who doesn't have a *son*. Where I am taken as a *person*, not just as a mere conduit to bring sons. Where I was not told to take *chances*.

Where I don't have to face demeaning remarks about feminism. Where having girls is not a matter of sorrow. Where I was provided with safe and strong contraception without being judged or insulted. Where my choices were respected. Where *I* mattered – my consent mattered; my emotional well-being mattered. Where I wasn't just a channel to bring babies to the world. Where my worth didn't depend on my motherhood choices.

Where I was given a voice and a say in my personal decisions, where nobody asked me *"Where are your elders?"* while offering contraception advice. Where I was treated as a grown-up. Where I could breathe and be myself.

Where there was a system in place to diagnose the symptoms of depression and anxiety in a would-be mother, where the healthcare staff picked up the signs of my serious prenatal and postnatal depression, where I was rescued from my suicidal tendencies, where me and my daughters remained safe.

I am grateful to this beautiful country, where I wasn't born but where I feel protected and sheltered.

I am grateful to this land which makes me want to call it *motherland.*

Chapter Fifty-Four

IN CASE YOU MISSED THE POINT

Just a few clarifications before I approach the end.

I am not against the idea of childbirth. I mean, how could I be? The existence of all of mankind is based on this very idea; you and I are alive and breathing just because childbirth exists.

You want to have children? Go on, have them and enjoy this journey by all means. In fact, we should all, including myself, be thankful to the mothers who are willing to have babies. They are the reason that we have this full-on world around us today, why we have siblings, friends, cousins, uncles and aunties, our favourite celebrities, musicians, authors and scientists and whatnot ... just because mothers were there to give birth to all these people.

Bravo!

Good on you!

Hats off!

Really heartfelt salute to all of you mothers out there!

What I'm against is the idea of a mother who is either *not willing* or *not prepared* being forced to have a child. It's risky, and in some cases it's fatal.

A woman's informed *consent* should be at the forefront of this whole process. That's what *she* deserves and that's what the *baby* deserves.

Secondly, I'm not against someone wishing to have a son. It is a noble wish, just like many other noble wishes; just like any other wish that aims to harm no one. And it's true, prophets wished for sons and God didn't mind them doing so – in fact, He granted the wishes of many.

What I oppose here is the approach with which this wish is enforced and then reinforced, over and over again.

That whole process is demeaning and exhausting, and suffocating for women who are being subjected to this wish.

Evaluate your means, see how many kids you can afford to raise and then leave the rest to God. Be content with His decisions and stop torturing your women, your daughters/daughters-in-law in the name of this noble wish, lest it become *vicious* instead of noble.

Celebrate every child regardless of its gender; that's what I'm advocating for.

Thirdly, I am not a feminist. Even though I oppose the oppression against women just as a feminist does, there is a fundamental difference between the two of us.

A feminist asks for equality. With equality comes equal rights and equal obligations. A woman should work and earn and be the equal partner of her male counterpart and so much more. She is to be treated in an equal manner too.

In the realm of feminism, a non-working woman is *not* considered as *productive* as one who is working, she is tagged as *mum at home* or *housewife,* which we all know are derogatory phrases. Feminism has robbed women of the pride of being a full-time wife or mother. Women these days feel embarrassed to admit that they are *only* mothers and not doing much besides that.

I want all the rights and privileges that my religion guarantees us. I want a woman to be respected for the mere fact that she is a woman. I want men to lower their gaze when approached by a woman. I want them to offer her a seat when she is standing on a busy bus or train or any public place. I want her to be provided for. I want her to own and inherit property. I want her to keep her name if she so wishes. I want her to make her motherhood choices as she pleases. I want her to feel respected for her choices. I want her to have access to education and to be able to work. And on the same note, I want her to work only if she *wants/needs* to work. I do not want the *obligation* of earning; I want the *choice* and the *ability*.

I want to see women as strong as Khadija (AS), who was a tradeswoman and was able to support her husband financially in times of need, and I want the men as supportive as Mohammad (PBUH), who loved and respected his wife and who welcomed his daughter wholeheartedly.

Feminism gives me less … Islam gives me more. I want more.

Now let's move to the end.

Chapter Fifty-Five

DO NOT PASS THE PARCEL

In birthday parties here in Australia, kids play a game called "pass the parcel". There is a parcel full of surprises, and each surprise gift is wrapped up in a layer of the parcel. All the kids sit in a circle and keep passing the parcel while the music is being played. When the music stops, whoever is holding the parcel takes his surprise gift by unwrapping one layer. *One has to keep passing the parcel as long as the music is being played.*

We are surrounded by evil norms and fake social values in society. It may not appear this way to us, but the truth is that we do have a say in them … we do have a choice.

A norm comes to us in a *pass the parcel* style, we get it from our forefathers and pass it on. The moment we get the *parcel*, we have the power to make a difference. That is our *power* … that is the choice. If the *parcel* is ugly we can choose to throw it away and not pass it on. This choice is hard at times, I admit – very hard, in fact. It requires one to stand alone. It requires one to possess the courage to break the chain of action taken by generations and even by all contemporaries. It requires one to have the ability to withstand the criticism, isolation, sarcasm, demeaning comments and even severe penal actions in many cases. It's an act of rebellion to start with, and we all know rebels are never welcomed.

If we look around or look back, it was the rebels who brought all sorts of reforms that we see in our world today, be it social, political, religious or philosophical. Mohammad (PBUH) and Jesus (AS) and Moses (AS), Noah (AS), Ibrahim (AS) were the rebels of their times. Nelson Mandela, Martin Luther King, Che Guevara, Harriet Tubman, Robert Owen, Jane Addams were rebels of different times. The list is long and we all know that. We all know that every hero who we look up to today was once labelled as a rebel. As Oscar Wilde said, "Disobedience, in the eyes of anyone who has read history, is man's original virtue. It is through disobedience that progress has been made, through disobedience and rebellion." So that's the one choice that we as human beings can make.

We have another choice: simply pass the parcel. It's easy, acceptable, popular and trendy. That's why most people make this choice, and the cycle of evil norms goes on and on…

I received a parcel saying "no contraception advice for children when they reach the age of marriage, it's too shameful to give such a word to your children".

I see no logic or sensibility in this particular norm. If my kids deserve advice from me on their food choices, on

176

health, on schooling and education, on travelling, on social aspects of life, on relationships, on household and cooking, on career paths, on emotional matters … then why the hell should I leave them alone on the family planning aspect of life? Why should I leave them in dark? How could I?

So, I'm going to break this parcel and throw it out of their range.

I have also received this other norm from the society where I grew up: "I wish you have a boy … oh, you have a girl … don't worry, I'll pray for you next time it'll be a boy Insha'Allah."

This sugar-coated, religion-coated, gentle and harmless looking evil norm's parcel has also come to me, and I have decided to throw it out of my life … my home … my household … and definitely far away from my girls. I will never whisper this thing into their ears, because I know the implications and connotations attached to it. I know the repercussions and ramifications it entails, I know the distress and misery it can cause. I know this whole idea inside out, and I know how ugly it can be. I know that this sweet-looking wish expressed with deep sighs will snatch away my girls' self-esteem. It will give them the impression that they are not worthy, not good enough. I won't let that parcel go beyond me.

I acknowledge that not all of you can do what I chose to do. Many of you don't have the power or means or authority or affordability to take daring steps like these.

I acknowledge that for many women, it's merely a choice between two difficult options.

Many women choose to have a baby or another baby or babies not because they want to, not because it's affordable, not because it's safe, but merely because they might have to face financial abuse, physical abuse, social abuse, divorce, homelessness or even worse, having to live without their children or even death.

While my heart bleeds for those women who are facing one form of abuse or other, it also feels enraged for those who have the power and ability to make a better choice, but still don't.

All of us lucky ones who have this opportunity and willingness to break the chain of ugly *parcels* are doing a favour to those who can't. We are changing the trend … we are setting the trend.

A few decades ago, my parents received a few parcels from their forefathers, namely:

"Don't educate girls."

"Don't let them travel alone."

"Don't let them work."

"Don't let them drive."

"Don't make them too bold."

"Don't give them wings," and so on …

Now this couple, who weren't highly educated – they both grew up in a rural, norm-ruled society – they could have followed suit. They could keep those parcels and passed them on as obedient servants of society. That option was easy, smooth, acceptable and hassle free.

But they decided to do something daring instead. They stood up and threw all those ugly stinky parcels far, far away from the lives of their daughters.

They were scolded, admonished, criticised. They were told time and again that they were doing something highly risky, shameful and bad.

They listened, but paid no heed ...

They educated us, they let us work and travel and drive. They did not label us as *weak* or *a burden.* They named us as *colour* and *joy* of their home.

They gave us wings to fly ...

In my case I actually physically flew ... from Pakistan to Australia.

They gave me wings and the strength to fly and rescue my family.

Now I don't have to worry about those ugly parcels, and neither do my sisters. My daughters won't even get a clue that there was such a parcel once in their ancestors' lives.

That couple's daring act rescued the generations from ignorance and illiteracy.

The good news is that many, if not all – at least the ones who have awareness and consciousness, and those who have some courage, especially the educated younger generation out there – we are capable of breaking the chains of ugly norms; those horrible parcels that are robbing the happiness from millions and millions. If we just refuse to be obedient servants of society we can do it ... we can bring happiness to our own homes, to our society.

And remember, anything that we don't take care of, our daughters will have to.

Let the music play ... do not pass the parcel.

Just in Case

Most of the helplines listed below are from services that are run in New South Wales; please contact your local community legal centre to find out about the services in your own state/near your area.

Pregnancy, Birth and Baby helpline – Call 1800 882 436

https://www.pregnancybirthbaby.org.au

The Pregnancy, Birth and Baby Helpline supports parents on the journey from pregnancy, to baby and pre-school. Guidance and reassurance is offered about behavioural and developmental concerns such as tantrums, walking, talking or reading for children up to five years of age.

Suicide Prevention Number – Lifeline – Call 13 11 14

Lifeline is a national charity providing all Australians experiencing a personal crisis with access to 24-hour crisis support and **suicide prevention** services.

Family violence – Aboriginal Contact Line 1800 019 123

(8 am to 6 pm, Monday to Friday)

This service provides information, support and referrals to other agencies that can help a victim of family violence.

Victims Access Line (VAL)

8 am to 6 pm, Monday to Friday 1800 633 063

Sydney metropolitan area (02) 8688 5511

Provides information and support if one is having problems getting application forms or needs help filling in counselling or financial support applications.

Women's Domestic Violence Court Advocacy Services (WDVCAS)

Call 1800 WDVCAS (1800 938 227)

Break Your Silence,

Stop the Violence

Women's Domestic Violence Court Advocacy Services (WDVCAS) are local, community based organisations in NSW. They assist women and kids at court and can provide help and support in obtaining an Apprehended Violence Order (AVO). They are funded by Legal Aid NSW.

Domestic Violence Legal Service

(02) 8745 6999 (Sydney area)

1800 810 784 (outside Sydney)

1.30 pm – 4.30 pm – Monday and Thursday

9.30 am – 12.30 pm – Tuesday and Friday

This is a state-wide legal service for women who are experiencing domestic violence. Subject to availability, the service is able to represent women applying for Apprehended Violence Orders.

Sydney Multicultural Community Services

(02) 9663 3922 Monday–Friday 8.30 am – 5.00 pm

www.sydneymcs.org.au

Provides information, resources and referral services for culturally and linguistically diverse community members.

Immigrant Women's Speakout Association

(02) 9635 8022 Monday–Friday 9.30 am – 5.00 pm

www.speakout.org.au

This is the peak advocacy, information, referral and research body for immigrant and refugee women in New South Wales. The Association also provides direct services in the area of domestic violence.

The Asylum Seekers Centre of NSW

(02) 9078 1900 Monday–Thursday 9.00 am – 4.00 pm

www.asylumseekerscentre.org.au

Provides practical support for community-based asylum seekers living in greater metropolitan Sydney.

Domestic Violence Hotline

1800 65 64 63 (24 hours)

A counselling and referral service run by specially trained professionals for people experiencing or escaping violence from a partner or ex-partner. The service also provides information on applying for an Apprehended Domestic Violence Order.

NSW Rape Crisis Centre

1800 424 017 (24 hours)

www.nswrapecrisis.com.au

Provides counselling and information services, and telephone crisis, support and referral service.

1800RESPECT: Domestic Violence and Sexual Assault National Helpline

1800 200 526 (24 hours)

Provides information and support referrals for people experiencing violence. This service can also assist friends and family who want to know how they can help.

Victims Services NSW

(02) 8688 5511 (Sydney metropolitan)

1800 633 063 (24 hours)

www.lawlink.nsw.gov.au/vs

Provides confidential emotional support and information regarding compensation for victims of crime.

Women's Legal Service NSW

(02) 9749 5533 (Sydney area)

1800 801 501 (outside Sydney)

Monday, Tuesday, Thursday and Friday

9.30 am – 4.30 pm

www.womenslegalnsw.asn.au

Provides women with free legal advice and assistance to find legal representation.

WEAVE

(02) 9699 9036 Monday to Friday 9.30 am –4.30 pm

www.weave.org.au

Works with mothers from culturally and linguistically diverse backgrounds to help them obtain a range of support services.

Australian Chinese Community Association of NSW

(02) 9281 1377

Monday to Friday 9.00 am – 5.00 pm

Saturday 9.00 am – 3.00 pm

www.acca.org.au

Provides community services to the Australian Chinese community, including counselling and assistance with personal and family problems.

First Light Care

(02) 9211 9988

Monday to Friday 9.30 am – 5.00 pm

www.firstlightcare.org.au

Provides family counselling for members of the Australian Chinese Community.

Muslim Women Association

(02) 9750 6916

Monday to Friday 9.00 am – 5.00 pm

www.mwa.org.au

Provides information, outreach support, counselling referrals and crisis accommodation.

For those in Pakistan

Having been away from Pakistan for more than a decade now, I am not aware of many services/helplines. I have, however, managed to find a few organisations working for social justice.

Kashf Foundation

Serving all with dignity by providing high-quality and sustainable microfinance services to low-income families and micro-entrepreneurs to enhance financial capabilities, alleviate household poverty and enable all, especially women, to become active agents of social and economic change.

(I am a personal fan of this organisation, as it is helping many women become financially self-reliant. Financial instability forms the basis for many other forms of abuse. In many cases, financial dependence prevents women from walking free from abuse.)

92 - 42 35248916

92 - 42 111 981 981

info@kashf.org

Taskeen

A not-for-profit organisation working for health and wellbeing of Pakistani citizens. It is also running a very active social media campaign called #DilKholo, where people share stories of their suffering and survival from different forms of abuse.

92 - 316 8275336

http://www.taskeen.org/

Super Abbu

A helpline connecting expectant fathers to doctors.

Superabbu.com

92 - 42 38900801

92 - 42 3890-0807

formulation

Acknowledgments

Thank you, Daddy and Ammi, for giving me wings to fly. Thank you for all the sacrifices and hard times that you both went through in the process of giving us a better and brighter life, while living in the midst of a patriarchal and tough society.

Thank you Mian Jee (my maternal grandfather) for being what you were, for passing on the genes of sensitivity and creativity in me. I don't see them coming from anyone but you.

Thank you Sadi for reminding me what a friendship feels like. I had forgotten the taste of friendship a long time ago. It was your arrival in my life that made me feel alive again. Thank you for encouraging me while I was working on this book.

Thank you, Ammar, for being there in all the dark moments of my life, you are a glow worm that shines in the dark. Thank you for all the support you have provided in the process of writing this book.

Thank you, Liz Gilbert. You came again, while I was writing this , you locked me up from outside and sat there like a guard with a gun in your hand, you killed all the reasons that came to distract me/stop me/discourage me. You killed them all and kept me going. You came through your book *Big Magic* this time. Thank you for being such a supportive person.

Thank you, Shelley, for being such a supportive person. You let me have all the flexibility to keep working and then finishing this book while I was working for you. You proved that one can be a very nice person while being a boss: a rare occurrence though.

Thank you, Sidra, for doing such a beautiful translation for my poem that I have added in the chapter "Clip their wings". When I read the translation, my instant reaction "my God, was it even capable of being converted into these magical words of Shakespeare's style English?"

Thank you, Jamal. You joined me almost at the end of this project to help on the technical side that really was a big help. You let me bombard you with so many dumb questions without getting irritated; I truly feel grateful for that.

Thank you, Graeme Addicott, for making it feel like home in Australia, for making me and my daughters feel welcome, for being so kind and generous over the years. Thank you for showing me that there are people like you in this world who would choose to be kind to those from whom they expect no return. Thank you for proving to me that love is not a trade. Thank you for showing me that racists are all wrong. When you send emails to your children, you cc me in; you don't know how much it means to me at a time when I can't get emails from my daddy anymore, thank you for doing that.

Thank you, Bhai, for saying this to me in 2011 when I missed an enrolment:

"Pack your bags and leave Australia, you have no guts to fight here" … it kept me going. And then saying this to me in 2016 when I got admitted as a Solicitor: "I don't know about the rest of Australians, but if I have to choose, you are my Australian of the year."

Thank you, God, for all the love that you have shown me over the years through kind people who you kept sending towards me. I know I don't even qualify to say much about you but let me say this YOU ARE AWESOME AND I LOVE YOU.

Notes

Chapter 26

1. A line from Shakespeare's Macbeth